The Revelation Happened

How Mystery Babylon Destroyed Jerusalem and Crept into our Churches, Governments, Science, and Lives to Deceive Us All

Don Nordstrom

Copyright © 2021 by Don Nordstrom.
All rights reserved worldwide.

No part or in whole may be reproduced, stored in a retrieval system, transcribed or transferred by any mechanical or media means, except for brief quotations in printed reviews, without the prior written permission of Don Nordstrom.

All Scriptures are from the King James Bible, Public Version. Word definitions are from Strong's Exhaustive Concordance, Public Version.

The alleged historical contents in this book include over eighteen years of a comprehensive study. To enhance reader understanding, the author encourages everyone to research the findings presented.

Please refer to the original King James Bible (KJV). This version maintained certain words from the Jewish and Greek texts that bring out the original intent. If not available, many free KJV Bible resources are online.

Thank you for supporting the hard work from this remarkable historian and author.

Contents

Author's Note 1

Dedication 3

Introduction 5

Is There a True Religion? 9

Blending Religions with the Gospel 15

Covenants 21

The Start of the False Roman Church 23

Religion in Science—Intelligence and Time 31

From Dragons to Dinosaurs 37

What Are Babylonian Inspired Religions? 45

Then What Happened? 51

How Do Religions Honor Mystery Babylon? 55

How Can We Know What the True Church Is? 63

The Roman Empire and the Jewish Population 67

Preparing to Understand Revelation 75

Revelation 83

Revelation 2 91

Revelation 3 97

Revelation 4 103

Revelation 5 105

Revelation 6 107

Revelation 7 115

Revelation 8	117
Revelation 9	125
Revelation 10	131
Revelation 11	135
Revelation 12	143
Revelation 13	151
Revelation 14	159
Revelation 15	165
Revelation 16	167
Revelation 17	171
Revelation 18	177
Revelation 19	179
Revelation 20	181
Revelation 21–22	185
So Now What?	189
Acknowledgments	191

Author's Note

> *"And upon her forehead was a name written, Mystery, Babylon The Great, The Mother Of Harlots And Abominations Of The Earth."*
>
> **- *Revelation 17:5***

This verse is from the book of Revelation in the Bible. Most Bible teachers do not understand the impact this verse has on our world and on our lives. Only a few people understand that this book is one of the most important historical works of Scripture.

It is believed the apostle John (a personal witness of the risen Jesus), wrote the book while on the Isle of Patmos in the Aegean Sea. Historians say the Romans tried to silence him by banishment to Patmos. Before his isolation, he most likely taught about the risen Jesus in Asia Minor (modern-day Turkey).

It was at Patmos that he received a prophecy foretold in the Old Testament and by Jesus, which soon came upon the Jewish people.

Despite what writers and Bible teachers have told us about the "end times", Revelation and Mystery Babylon are understandable once we know the symbolism and the history. Much of Revelation is the fulfillment of Old Testament prophecy in symbolism and shows:

- a warning to seven churches about the mystic practices of Mystery Babylon,

- judgment upon the Jewish temple system and false Jews for bringing in this demonic controlled belief system,

- the end of the Old Testament age, and the eternal New Testament of the Holy Spirit baptized true church placed into action.

The major theme of Revelation shows us a spiritual court in session where a judge passes judgment on Israel-Judea and eternity. For centuries, God warned His people, the Jews, not to chase after strange gods, goddesses, or false beliefs.

The temple leadership had brought Mystery Babylon into their temple, and God allowed the destroyer to bring them to destruction in AD 70. Revelation contrasts Old Testament history with the restored kingdom of God released into the Spirit baptized true church, which He calls His bride.

Mystery Babylon is not the city of Babylon but a powerful, *deceiving*, and *controlling* belief system that started thousands of years ago. What this book shows is how this ancient power still deceives organized religions, influences our lives, and prevents us from knowing God's original plan—His spiritual kingdom baptized into us.

Dedication

To all the deceived people of the world...

"*And the great dragon was cast out, that old serpent, called the Devil, and Satan, <u>which deceiveth the whole world</u>: he was cast out into the earth, and his angels were cast out with him.*"
(Underline added)

– **Revelation 12:9**

Don Nordstrom

Introduction

"There are three things I have learned never to discuss with people: religion, politics, and the Great Pumpkin."

Charlie Brown

With all due respect to Charlie Brown, we need to consider religion, politics, and other subjects concerning the powers that deceive us, even metaphorically, the Great Pumpkin.

Deception first entered our young lives thanks to traditions from our parents and others. During our childhood, we believed in characters such as the Tooth Fairy, the Easter Bunny, Santa Claus, and in Charlie's case, the Great Pumpkin.

As we grew older, we discovered, to our dismay, that those stories were lies. Most of us also heard something similar to the Great Pumpkin—a being we believe exists, yet we cannot prove it, and we'll call this *the god of our religion*.

Sometimes deceptions at first seem innocent, and so we accept them. However, it left us to determine if the god of our religion was part of the deception.

Throughout history, people have created many gods and goddesses, idols, or beliefs that controlled their lives and explained their environment. But there are also groups that don't believe in gods or religions.

Others claim they've met an *uncreated*, loving God named Jesus. He taught that He came from a father-type Spirit in a spirit world where there is no time (eternity) as we perceive it.

How can this be? Is it possible to prove to ourselves, and others, that a spiritual realm (i.e., heaven or different universe) and a loving God exist outside our world of superstitious religions?

The irony is that religions have caused many people to become unbelievers, and the unbelievers' state that those who *do* believe in God are, well, blithering idiots.

To their point, do we want to waste our lives bobbing our heads, bowing up and down, singing the same chants, saying the same prayers, or anxiously rubbing beads? Should we hand over our hard-earned money to a religious TV salesperson? Is a camp meeting the place we need to send payment for a breakthrough of a hundred-fold blessing in return? Hasn't science proven our universe came from a big bang and evolved over billions of years? Didn't human organisms come from a mineral slime pool?

The answer to these questions is no. They are deceptions to knowing the certainty of God and His purpose for us.

Most children have heard a story where a kingdom exists, with a prince and a princess and a benevolent king who governs his realm. Evil, as a dark knight or a dragon, entered this world, put the princess under a spell, and the prince rescued her. It was the king's judgment of salvation (saving the princess) that overcame the evil, and his people lived happily ever after.

Deep within our spirit, there seemed a life of realism about this world. Boys imagined their princely rule and built forts, swung swords, and fought against their enemy. They needed to rescue a damsel in distress.

Girls daydreamed of being a princess and had tea parties with dolls, who were there to comfort her with emotional support and serve her princess needs as she dreamed of her future prince.

Then, at some point, it all blew up. Someone lied to us and implied we were not worthy of being a prince or princess.

We believed them; our sub-conscious memory still holds the tragedy of that day when we exchanged a kingdom of realism to become the damsel in distress needing the rescue.

Doesn't the world stop when a royal wedding occurs, and we give all attention to the marriage ceremony? Something within us still stirs this interest.

We need to find out if there is a kingdom with a loving king where we can live happily ever after, or else dismiss this also as a lie.

Therefore, we need to prove that not only do the king and kingdom exist, but also how we can discover it for ourselves with no lingering doubt. There is a book that tells us about it: the Bible.

We will find out how we can have a personal and dynamic relationship with a king named Jesus. The world's religions haven't told us this is freely available without living under their rules and controlling doctrines. Instead, they recruit members to serve their false doctrines and rules through religious and spiritual abuse. This is the primary reason there are unbelievers today.

Once we know how organized religions distort the truths about God and His Word, we become convinced that the Bible is not a book of fables.

We can find out:
- how religions promote the deceptions of Mystery Babylon,
- what the Bible is telling us,
- who started deception,
- how religious deceptions deceive us in our lives through science, politics, media, and the like,
- and, how we can fully understand the symbolism in the book of Revelation.

Don Nordstrom

Is There a True Religion?

Is there a true religion? The short answer is no. There are volumes of texts on religions throughout history and in the world. We will not chase down each one because we will discover they started from one belief system. Each created sect provided a style of living according to whichever unloving god *the religion* appeased.

Most people do not know there is a false religious Christianity and a non-religious true Christianity. Much of organized religion follows a false Christianity under their terms and not what the Bible teaches, which we will further explain.

Babylon started idol worship, which passed down into other countries through the centuries. Eventually, the Jewish people ignored God and brought Babylonian worship into their temple. This is what the book of Revelation describes as Mystery Babylon.

The Gnostic religion adopted Mystery Babylon by practicing pagan worship, along with adapting certain teachings from the apostles. The Roman religion then brought in this type of blended "Christian" religion, and it later passed down into the denominations.

Jesus did not start a religion, but a new *covenant relationship*. This covenant relationship is His true church through the Holy Spirit fire baptism starting at Pentecost.

He implied the old covenant or Old Testament (OT) Scriptures written throughout the centuries by Jewish scribes revealed who He was. Jesus started by teaching from the book of Isaiah:

> *The Spirit of the Lord is upon me, because he hath anointed me to preach the gospel to the poor; he hath sent me to heal the brokenhearted, to preach deliverance to the captives, and recovering of sight to the blind, to set at liberty them that are bruised, To preach the acceptable year of the Lord...*
> *And he began to say unto them, This day is this scripture fulfilled in your ears.*
>
> *– Luke 4:18-19,21*

Who did Jesus teach this to in the synagogues? The poor (always indebted to the temple, never learned the gospel [truth]); the brokenhearted (never met the loving God); the captives, or Jews (their minds controlled by false religious leaders); and the blind and bruised, because the greatest false religious gods of the time had them bound and abused (oppressed).

He was also teaching it to us because false religions have bound most of us today in tradition, keeping the world from knowing freedom from controlling gods (religious teachers). Among other reasons, He came to set us free from religions!

The temple rabbis (supposed Jewish master teachers of the Scriptures) had memorized the Torah or Law Scriptures but did not understand the rest of the old covenant, or otherwise they would have known their Savior—Jesus. The leaders became deceived through hundreds of their made-up oral laws (Talmud) and pagan beliefs, which they brought into the temple (Matthew 23).

Many religious teachers today *know* but do not *understand* what the Scriptures are saying, as they have allowed pagan mystic beliefs and traditions into their religions.

The temple leaders had learned from distorted doctrines how to control and fleece their followers. They placed obstacles between God and the Jews, which other organized religions still maintain more importance on saving their doctrines than revealing the kingdom of God through Jesus.

However, most religions tell us to believe in Jesus, because the New Testament (NT) states:

That if thou shalt confess with thy mouth the Lord Jesus, and shalt believe in thine heart that God hath raised him from the dead, thou shalt be saved.

- Romans 10:9

This is true, and the key is we "shall be saved" if we confess and believe with our innermost being that God raised Jesus from the dead.

But saved from what? And how can anyone confess someone we have never seen or met? Besides, this is what every idol worshiper, cult, or religion has as their requirement: to believe in their god.

Is there a different way to believe in Jesus beyond our senses? Is there a more intimate way to meet and know Him?

The overall theme of the OT is how the Lord God tried to get His elect, the Jewish people, to join into a spiritual covenant marriage with God. No matter what He did for them, they always broke their covenants. His people were unfaithful, chasing after false gods and beliefs. We still do this today, knowingly or not.

In the OT, God lays out His spiritual marriage in heartbreaking detail. His spiritual wife, Israel-Judah, acted as harlots:

And I saw, when for all the causes whereby backsliding Israel committed adultery I had put her away, and given her a bill of divorce; yet her treacherous sister Judah feared not, but went and played the harlot also.

- Jeremiah 3:8

Because the Jewish leaders killed their prophets and, later, the followers of Jesus, God had the false leaders' temple and Jerusalem destroyed in AD 70. We see Revelation lays this out in apocalyptic symbols—God divorcing Israel-Judea for His new bride or true church (NT).

Through God's "Son" *Jesus* (from Greek translation), or *Yehoshua* (Hebrew), or represented as *Jehovah*-LORD God (English translation of YHVH) of the OT, a new eternal marriage covenant became possible with *anyone* who would accept the Savior Jesus promised from the OT and NT (Isaiah 9:6, 43:11, John 3:16, 4:42).

Genesis chapters 1 and 2:4 combined with John 1 show us Jesus (as the *maker* of all things) was the Lord God in the OT.

What most churches teach is we still need to follow rules from an unworkable relationship in the old covenant. This is how they control their followers with added unnecessary rules and doctrines.

The OT can only teach us *why* the NT became necessary. But the OT is now obsolete, and we need to follow the teachings from Jesus, who is our new covenant or NT (Hebrews 8:12-13). Not only did Jesus save us from the Mystery Babylon religions, but also from our terminal disease–eternal judgment.

The NT explains that Jesus is the Son, or second person, of the divine Godhead family, which Jesus described as the Father, the Son, and the Holy Spirit. This unites them as one, as God.

Go ye therefore, and teach all nations, baptizing them in the name of the Father, and of the Son, and of the Holy Ghost.
(Name underlined to point out the singularity of all three as one divine being, God)

- Matthew 28:19

...To the acknowledgement of the mystery of God, and of the Father, and of Christ; in whom are hid all the treasures of wisdom and knowledge...
For in him dwelleth all the fulness of the Godhead bodily.

- Colossians 2:2,3,9

The words within the Bible are translations from a group of inspired Jewish texts and also translated into Greek. They document a dramatic human link with an *uncreated* God. He attempted several covenant relationships with His people only to have them break each one, destroying themselves and their children.

We discover how false, mystic beliefs from idols or gods, originating from Babylon, seduced the Jews away, and these mystic beliefs are alive today.

Don Nordstrom

Blending Religions with the Gospel

During the first AD centuries, the believers in Jesus accepted the Jewish and Greek texts as the inspired Word of God. However, there were arguments with other groups demanding an inclusion of their mystic philosophies or beliefs.

The NT of the Bible teaches that after Jesus' bodily resurrection, the apostles (those who witnessed His reappearance), now baptized with God's Spirit, showed how the kingdom of God had come and is now available *within us* to all who believe. They first traveled throughout the land to teach the Jews the good news of Jesus and His resurrection—their Savior, promised from the OT, had at last come.

The temple leaders' relentless persecution of the new church proved they were losing their ability to deceive their followers to worship the temple religion. There was no need to adhere to all the laws and rituals the false leaders created.

One of the worst persecutors, named Saul, was a Jewish-Roman who received a stunning change of heart. One day, he was on the road to Damascus to continue his attacks. Along the way, He met the risen Jesus through a spiritual experience. Jesus asked Saul why he was persecuting *Him*. Through a series of events, Saul converted and then learned everything about Jesus.

Because of his *personal* witness and transformation, he also became an apostle. His name changed to Paul, and he shared the teachings he received from the resurrected Jesus with the Gentiles (non-Jews) throughout the Roman Empire (primarily Rome).

Many of Paul's learned Gentiles came from pagan or Greek philosophies (Babylon inspired) and wanted to merge their beliefs in with their new teachings from Paul. One group, the Gnostic, believed they could achieve a better understanding through greater knowledge and our own mystical interpretation.

The basis of Gnosticism is that we don't need the Holy Spirit and can save our godlike selves with our own academic efforts (works). We can achieve this through illumination from secret mystical knowledge. Have we heard this before? The serpent preached a similar sermon in Eden. This practice still goes on today, some through secret groups. Many do not realize that the hidden or secret knowledge they are seeking is, in effect, worshiping Lucifer as Satan.

To help keep their spiritual teachings pure, the apostles elected certain elders to keep false doctrines out of their groups. Several leaders took the title of *bishop* (1st Timothy 3).

However, bishops were not apostles, and apostles were not bishops! This is where a deceiving doctrine began in the Roman Catholic religion. The apostle Peter was not the bishop of Rome or the first pope, as the idol-worshiping Roman religion had claimed.

Peter would have had nothing to do with an idol-worshiping church. Besides, Jesus did not build His church upon the apostle Peter (another false Catholic doctrine), which we will show later from the Bible.

Other leaders—not appointed by the apostles—called themselves bishops and wanted to unite their groups with their own mystic beliefs, in with the teachings of the apostles. Because of their efforts, they described themselves as universal or *catholic* (the Roman religion would later adopt the *Catholic* title).

These wolves in sheep's clothing tried to keep certain OT laws alive, blended with their mystic Babylonian inspired practices. It was a deceptive way to control and rule over their followers. These are still in practice today, as many leaders do not know the difference between the OT and the NT.

But the converted "virgin" Christians, Spirit-baptized from the apostles, believed none of the doctrines from men. God's Spirit now led His church. This was His plan from the start and still is today.

Baptism in the Holy Spirit differs from baptism in water. Before Jesus came, water baptism was symbolic, first performed on cleansing temple priests and later, on others by John the Baptist.

Full dunking of the body in water baptism from John represented separation, repentance, and washing away of sins. It was a testimonial display to show that Jesus would come in our stead. He would die for us, take all of our unfaithfulness and evil (sinful) nature into death, and then rise again to lead us into a new life. However, instead of water, His shed blood would forever wash away our sins.

John was prophesying the coming of Jesus, where Jesus's shed blood would wash away the sins for His church. Now, with the covenant-shed blood, a believer's baptism is in the Holy Spirit, as John the Baptist testified:

I indeed baptize you with water unto repentance. but he that cometh after me is mightier than I, whose shoes I am not worthy to bear: he shall baptize you with the Holy Ghost, and with fire:
(underline added)

– Matthew 3:11

Religions believe in a religious god, with false doctrines and rules. People create Christianity on their terms. They perform ritualistic works, putting faith in their religion, instead of trusting Jesus from His Spirit baptism.

Some still believe water baptism from OT Jewish tradition is necessary to become a Christian. Whereas, to *know* our baptism comes from the Holy Spirit, who comes to dwell within us.

As Jesus said:

And I will pray the Father, and he shall give you another Comforter, that he may abide with you forever; Even the Spirit of truth; whom the world cannot receive, because it seeth him not, neither knoweth him: but ye know him; for he dwelleth with you, and shall be in you.

– John 14:16-17

Jesus answered and said unto him, If a man love me, he will keep my words: and my Father will love him, and we will come unto him, and make our abode with him.

– John 14:23

But the Comforter, which is the Holy Ghost, whom the Father will send in my name, he shall teach you all things, and bring all things to your remembrance, whatsoever I have said unto you.

– John 14:26

The only leading we need is listening to the words of Jesus and the apostles in the NT, and through His Spirit. Once a person receives the Holy Spirit, they become born again, and will have His Spirit and kingdom forever. Early believers could not deny their Spirit conversion, despite many imprisoned, tortured, and put to death.

Temple leaders would often stone to death or turn the newly baptized believers over to the Romans for tortures and crucifixion. The true church could not deny knowing Jesus as God, who was now making His kingdom alive in them.

This true church is available to all skeptics, agnostics, atheists, or others who may have suffered spiritual, physical, or sexual abuse from their religion, and can now find eternal peace with God.

Don Nordstrom

Covenants

There have been many covenants created throughout history. We still have them in families, real estate transactions, marriages, and contracts. Covenants were between two or more parties. They comprised strengths and weaknesses, promises, conditions, oaths, or shed blood, which gave life to the covenant.

The parties or families documented everything concerning their covenant and then had an exchange of assets; the two families became one, and their family names combined.

For example, perhaps one family named Nord was excellent farmers, and another family named Strom was skilled warriors. They could enter a covenant where the farmers fed the warriors and their families, and the warriors protected the farmer's fields and family. Their families became as one, took care of each other, and could then intermarry their names, such as Nordstrom.

In typical tribal covenants, shed blood occurred between the two-family leaders. They would slit a cut in their palms and then bound their hands together to intermingle their blood into each other's bodies. Other times, the leaders would sacrifice an animal (or more), split it down the middle, and the family leaders would stand in the blood as they swore their oaths to each other (Genesis 15 and 17). Abram's name changed to Abraham.

While united in the blood, they would exchange oaths, promises, and conditions. The conditions included the punishments for breaking the covenant, which were severe.

A covenant meant that the other family was more important than their personal family. This is where the saying, "Blood is thicker than water," came from—that is, the shed blood covenant was more important than the mother's water, shed at the birth of her children.

Today, we use ink instead of blood to create our contracts or covenants. At marriage weddings, there is a dinner eaten usually from slaughtered animals. In the marriage bed, the virgin woman would shed blood (not always true today), to complete their marriage covenant.

The covenants God made with Abraham and His people seemed one-sided because God had everything, and His selected people had nothing of value. The only assets man possessed were guilt, fear, shame, hatred, disobedience, sickness, deception, and so on.

God would take our hatred and give us love, take our fear and give us security, take our sickness and give us health, take our spiritual death and give us eternal life, take our deception and give us eternal truth.

The Jews just needed to accept the blessings and conditions God offered and follow His will. Although they broke each covenant, He would restore another covenant with His people, eventually making an eternal covenant with anyone who would accept it through the shed blood of Jesus. Thanks to *our* LORD God, Jesus, we can now return to carry out what He had planned for us from the beginning.

The Start of the False Roman Church

The Roman emperors had claimed their deity as gods from the advent of Caesar as god (the religion of *imperial cult*). The Romans whipped, sent to prison, or crucified those who refused to worship the emperor as a god (burning incense) or pay tribute (offerings or taxes) to Caesar.

When the true church spread throughout the empire, denying the Caesars as their gods, these tortures increased. The Romans slaughtered Spirit-baptized Christians in horrific circus-like displays of death. The Roman Catholic Church would later resume these tortures and deaths when Jews or true Christians refused to honor their false doctrines and church.

One of these earlier false doctrines claimed the apostle Simon Peter was in Rome for at least twenty-five years, acting as the bishop of Rome and the first pope. But the Bible says nothing about Peter in Rome.

There is evidence the apostle Paul was in Rome for many years. He identifies those with him and greets many people in his letters from Rome. If Peter was ever there, Paul, in his epistles or another of the NT books, would have mentioned it at least once.

There was another Simon whom some believe went to Rome and influenced forming doctrines now used by the false church. Peter had already met him in Samaria and perceived he was evil.

But there was a certain man, called Simon, which beforetime in the same city used sorcery, and bewitched the people of Samaria, giving out that himself was some great one: To whom they all gave heed, from the least to the greatest, saying, This man is the great power of God. And to him they had regard, because that of long time he had bewitched them with sorceries. But when they believed Philip preaching the things concerning the kingdom of God, and the name of Jesus Christ, they were baptized, both men and women.

Then Simon himself believed also: and when he was baptized, he continued with Philip, and wondered, beholding the miracles and signs which were done.

Now when the apostles which were at Jerusalem heard that Samaria had received the word of God, they sent unto them Peter and John: Who, when they were come down, prayed for them, that they might receive the Holy Ghost: (For as yet he was fallen upon none of them: only they were baptized in the name of the Lord Jesus.)

Then laid they their hands on them, and they received the Holy Ghost.

And when Simon saw that through laying on of the apostles' hands the Holy Ghost was given, he offered them money, Saying, Give me also this power, that on whomsoever I lay hands, he may receive the Holy Ghost.

> *But Peter said unto him, Thy money perish with thee, because thou hast thought that the gift of God may be purchased with money. Thou hast neither part nor lot in this matter: for thy heart is not right in the sight of God.*
>
> *Repent therefore of this thy wickedness, and pray God, if perhaps the thought of thine heart may be forgiven thee. For I perceive that thou art in the gall of bitterness, and in the bond of iniquity.*
>
> *Then answered Simon, and said, Pray ye to the Lord for me, that none of these things which ye have spoken come upon me.*
>
> – **Acts 8:9–24**

Three things, other than Simon the sorcerer, stand out in these verses. We read that despite the deceptions from Simon; the Samarians believed in Philip's teaching of Jesus (v. 12).

The second event was their baptism, probable water baptism from Jewish practice, or outward display of their intent to believe Jesus, instead of Simon the sorcerer.

The third is that the apostles, Peter and John, prayed and laid hands on them to receive the Holy Spirit (vv. 15–17). This shows there is a difference in water and Holy Spirit baptisms.

After Simon noticed the apostles were doing miracles (appearing as magic to Simon), he wanted that power for his own.

Simon wanted Peter to pray for him, but we are each responsible and accountable for our *repenting*, asking for forgiveness, and not by having membership in an organization or religion do it for us.

Historians then state, instead of repenting, this sorcerer Simon took the title of Simon Magus, meaning *magi* or *magician*. There is little doubt he engaged the Gnostic religion or blended pagan and Christian doctrines.

He was in Samaria, which already combined Jewish and Babylonian worship of gods (2 Kings 17:29-41). Some historians claim he took up with a prostitute, Helen of Tyre, who became a sexually energized female goddess, and who could be the "Jezebel" mentioned in Revelation.

The Romans called their supreme male gods *Pater* (Father), and it is easy to see how the title *Pater* could change to *Simon Pater Magus* as people titled him "the great power of God." Simon Pater Magus became Simon Peter.

Simon Magus thought that if he could have purchased an apostleship with the Holy Spirit "magic", he could add to his followers. Instead, he chose his mysticism to deceive people. This is the "bond of iniquity" the apostle Peter saw. (The Catholics would later call purchasing a leadership in their church *simony*).

Researchers then say Simon Magus went to Rome, which already had polytheism (multi-god worship). This false Simon Peter would sow the seeds for a universal, or catholic, church. The false church would name *this* Simon the bishop and first pope of Rome.

In AD 285, long after Simon Magus planted his mystic-catholic roots into Rome, the empire became so vast it divided into east (Byzantine empire) and west (later, the false church would also divide into east and west in 1053).

Between AD 311–315, the senior emperor, Galerius, along with the emperors Constantine and Licinius, put a stop to religious persecution through the Edict of Toleration and the Edict of Milan.

Constantine's mother, Helena, adopted *religious* mystic Christian worship as her religion, and her son, Constantine, did so later in life. They, and other Romans, only knew this as a better worship over other pagan deities, because they could worship all their gods at the same time.

Their imperialism invested heavily into religious temples, building cathedrals, basilicas, and monuments over supposed sacred areas of worship. This practice soon spread throughout the empire.

Constantine kept his worship of a sun god, Sol Invictus. He then changed the Jewish Sabbath "day of no work" on Saturday to SUN-day to keep his worship alive. This pagan god, Sol, still shines as a sunburst halo behind Catholic idols, carvings, pictures of Jesus and popular saints, and religious artwork.

In addition, Constantine ordered markets and public offices closed on Sundays. Few people know that a Roman emperor changed the Sabbath day of rest to worship Sol on Sunday and closed our public offices and financial markets on Sunday. Going to church on a Sunday has nothing to do with Jesus or the true church but the worship of a sun god.

There never was a special day to worship God, as the apostles and followers were in a spiritual church every day with the Lord Jesus, who is now our Sabbath of rest (Hebrews 4).

In AD 325, Constantine ordered bishops from around the empire to meet at Nicaea to organize their beliefs. The main discussion revolved around the deity of Jesus.

A pagan group, called Arians, argued that God created Jesus, whereas the Bible claimed He made all things, and was always with God as His wisdom or Word (John 1:1–3).

This council also drafted the Nicene Creed, the date for the Roman Easter, and set up canon law or church ordinances and regulations. Around AD 380, the bishops formalized the Nicene Creed, and the Edict of Thessalonica made Nicene Christianity beliefs as the state religion.

Constantine had died in AD 335, so now Emperor Theodosius started closing pagan temples while promoting the newer Roman religion. The door opened to bring in their idol and sun worship, mysticism, and mother-of-God worship (from the Queen of Heaven pagan worship) and further develop the universal church—the Roman Catholic Church.

The western Roman Empire soon came under foreign attack, and the government dwindled. This gave rise for popish authority to take sole command. A one-pope-emperor ruler lasted until around AD 800, when Pope Leo III proclaimed Charlemagne as a new emperor. Together they formed the Holy Roman Empire, which lasted until Napoleon dismantled it around 1800.

With their mystic-catholic and idol-worshiping traditions intact, the false Roman church would read only certain texts from the Vulgate in Latin. This kept the members poor, brokenhearted, captive, blind, and bruised (oppressed) to what the Bible and the words from Jesus said.

What we need to realize is the revived Roman Empire (there is nothing holy about it) still controls our lives through false doctrines, rules, and regulations. Despite claims from popes (and their historians) that their religion gave us our Bible and started the Christian church, we now see it is ridiculous.

In the 14th century, an Oxford professor named John Wycliffe translated the Roman Latin Vulgate into an old English New Testament. Eventually, more Bibles became available for everyone to read, and people realized how the false church had deceived them. This false Roman religion still promotes their church traditions over the Bible.

Instead of Roman crucifixions, the Catholic religion abused children, caused the slaughtering of countless Jews and true Christians, and burned martyrs at the stake—those who had the courage to stand up with boldness and deny that the Romans had established the true church.

God bless the "heretics" throughout history, who rose against the Roman Catholic Church to their tortured deaths. They now rule with God in His kingdom.

Parents do not realize they are endangering their children. This perverted religion still protects countless predators and pedophiles masquerading as priests and leaders who torture and sexually abuse children around the world.

But whoso shall offend one of these little ones which believe in me, it were better for him that a millstone were hanged about his neck, and that he were drowned in the depth of the sea.

– **Matthew 18:6**

The Roman Catholic religion deceived millions of people, and still does today, through the revived idol-worshiping Roman Empire, disguised as a Christian church.

God canonized the Scriptures through His Holy Spirit in the minds and hearts of true believers before this false church ever organized.

Don Nordstrom

Religion in Science—Intelligence and Time

Evolutionary Professor: "It took billions of years to make a human being."
Inquiring student: "Then why does it only take nine months now?"

Two main creation belief systems exist. One is biblical, where an uncreated God made all things. The other comes from ancient Babylon, where everything came together through created gods. This latter belief isn't obvious in our world at first until we dig deeper.

Sciences tell us that macro-evolution of the cosmos, chemicals, stars and planets, organisms, and micro-evolution created all things over billions of years. To their credit, so-called micro-evolution such as like-kind animal evolution is observable among domesticated pets or animals. However, it did not occur over billions of years, but from our breeding manipulation or loss of genetic information.

What if true Bible scholars and scientists sat down in a conference and looked at each other's findings? They would find glaring errors in both of their discoveries. Both religion and science are guilty of preexisting bias or assumptions, and these are not accurate Bible translations or accurate means of scientific investigations.

For many years, false religions had blocked or claimed scientists had committed heresy in their discoveries. One popular example would be Galileo, who, with his telescope, discovered the earth rotated around the sun. This went against the Roman religion who, out of context and mistranslation, stated the Bible said the sun rotated around the earth, which the Bible didn't say.

The fact is, the Roman religion created false doctrines by not understanding that the Jewish scribes wrote much of the Bible in God inspired symbolism and many religions still believe it is all literal and teach the same today.

Galileo had to reword his thesis at his inquisition in order to avoid torture or death. This was probably the beginning when scientists began seriously doubting the Roman religion along with the Bible. However, there is some commonality between the Bible and sciences.

The Bible stated the earth was circular (not flat) and the heavens were stretching (expanding universe) centuries before explorers and astrophysicists discovered it to be true (Isaiah 40:22). It implies there are two or more universes or realms (heavens), one we call the spiritual realm. Science is now letting on that they theorize a "multiverse", or more than one universe. Some even think there is a parallel universe.

If we can understand there is more than one realm or universe, then we can see why some things appear to be millions or billions of years old. Is it possible all things first formed in the timeless spiritual realm and then flushed out certain elements into making our universe?

Admittedly, this book is not a science journal, and not intended to prove or disprove scientists. However, a scientist is not exempt from the Babylonian inspired deceptions, and neither is anyone else. We can still come together with a better understanding of creation. One realm has existed forever, and ours, in relationship, just began.

Science has unconsciously accepted a mystic Mother Nature (Queen of Heaven) type theory that through hit or miss or trial and error or survival of the fittest over billions of years, created everything we see today.

Certain religions and sciences teach everything came from nothing or almost nothing, but neither one is true. What we see and experience today has always existed, *except* in a different format.

Everything existed eternally in the spiritual realm until something happened in God's kingdom that set it on a cycle of darkness and destruction. He created our universe to dump or flush the darkness and destruction out of His kingdom into our current realm (Genesis 1:2). More on that later, but we need to realize God never meant for us to exist eternally in *our* temporary physical realm.

When both arguments accept the discovery of intelligent *encoded* DNA, we can uncover creation. DNA involves the codes used in developing and maintaining organisms such as our bodies.

Evolution and creation from *nothing* then become a deception because it is impossible to send and receive codes (encoded communication) without having *intelligent* planning on both ends.

A person stranded on an island can transmit ABCD forever, without rescue. But change it to SOS, and help is coming. An intelligent *person created* the SOS Morse code, and the sender and receiver know what the encoded communication means to produce the desired outcome.

An intelligent *being made* all things (Genesis 2:4, John 1:1-4), and all physical organisms through DNA.

There is good science and imperfect science. Good science takes a subject, not knowing the outcome, and through repeated observation and testing, it comes up with the same proven result.

Bad science takes an unknown subject, assuming a result, and then goes out of its way with made up assumptions to prove the unknown result, whether or not the subject or result is even possible. This is the Mystery Babylon deception prominent in science today. We will see later how bad religion promotes Mystery Babylon.

Charles Darwin, knowingly or not, adopted a Babylonian Queen of Heaven creation belief system we call Mother Nature, just as many deceived scientists practice today. This belief is mystical in interpretation, which allows impossible assumptions in their theories.

Darwin looked at other scientists as gods, perhaps even Aristotle:

> *"From quotations I had seen I had a high notion of Aristotle's merits, but I had not the most remote notion what a wonderful man he was. Linnaeus and Cuvie have been my two gods, though in very different ways, but they were mere schoolboys to old Aristotle."* [1]

After examining beak variations with certain birds, Darwin used his developed mysticism and believed these birds grew or evolved unique beaks to survive in their separate environment—meaning bigger beaks for bigger seeds and smaller beaks for smaller seeds.

Removing this deception, the birds formed their beaks from either interbreeding with other birds—or they always existed this way and flew to different areas on their own or came by travelers. With more effort, little beaks can eat bigger seeds, and bigger beaks can eat smaller seeds. It is whatever is more convenient or available, not evolving for survival.

Now, through DNA investigation we know, for example, a canine Chihuahua dog came from a canine wolf. But it wasn't a matter of evolutionary survival. We also know this because of recorded history, where people over thousands of years used selective interbreeding of wolves into dogs. We have these varied forms of like-kind animals from interbreeding. Good science.

Evolution teaches that through need or survival, an organism or animal gains or turns on genes to make a different beak, or a wolf could change into a dog.

This assumption occurs from natural selection, or survival of the fittest, to adapt a beak or become a dog. Macro evolution also teaches an organism with lesser genes can evolve or jump to a more complex organism. If this was true, the Chihuahua, for example, could gain genes or DNA to become a human being. Bad science.

The arguments couldn't be more polarized. Either an organism started out having everything they needed to survive—or nothing split with something, which is impossible, and everything simply by chance came into being without a cause.

Admittedly, Darwin didn't understand genetics as we do today, but why does science continue teaching and preaching his myths?

It is obvious; certain wolves had some of their genetic DNA links corrupted, perhaps from diet, disease, or environment, which then passed on to their pups. We then interbred these wolves into dogs. This is how all animals or organisms came to be as they are today, through corrupted genetically encoded DNA and interbreeding with their own kind.

It is futile to believe simpler forms of life (macro) evolved or jumped to other forms on their own (e.g., apes evolved into humans). Death does not use mysticism or nature to make intelligence or encoded DNA. From this we know, which came first, the chicken or the egg. It is obvious Jesus made the chicken with an egg already inside.

Some believe many of our genes are dormant or we carry "junk" genes because they do not know their function. In the beginning, we had a purpose for all of our genes. They were necessary for living in a much different, eternal, spiritual world. We lost the information (became corrupt) when we turned from the light of God into darkness, and we became a lower form of being than what God intended for us.

Never were we supposed to live in our current physical realm, where all things eventually dissolve, corrupt, rust, decay, breakdown, destruct, die, and return into molecular dusts.

From Dragons to Dinosaurs

As children, we believed in the Tooth Fairy, the Easter Bunny, and Santa Claus. Today, a child experiences a separate and an even greater deception, and it is at the start of children's and science books:

"Millions of years ago, dinosaurs roamed the earth."

It is from this one sentence that has ignited the greatest deception from the science community. *Dinosaur* is a made-up word, *Dinosauria*, which comes from two Greek words: *deinos* (terrible or fearfully large) and *saurus* (lizard), or "huge, scary lizard".

Sir Richard Owen coined the term *dinosaur (huge, scary lizard)* in 1842. He was a British scientist who studied anatomy and fossils. Owen wanted a specific term or category for three particularly large-boned reptiles, which he discovered buried in Southern England and had presumed extinct.

This event occurred during Darwin's development of his theory of evolution, and the debate of natural selection over creation was coming to a scientific head.

It is probable that Owen was a theist (believed in God as some scientist's still did) because he at first took issue with Darwin's theory.

In the past, there had already been a term for dinosaurs—*dragons*. This catchall term, *dragons*, included serpents, and the Bible describes them thirty-four times. Historical documents also mentioned dragons and were in reports from explorers.

With many historical *dinosaur/dragon* documents available, it was difficult for the evolutionary scientists of the day (and should be today) to convince people that dinosaurs died out eons ago before humans came to be. After all, dinosaurs couldn't have existed millions of years ago with evidence to the contrary of relative recent sightings.

Therefore, the Bible and dragons had to become a myth. Dinosaurs as dragon artwork on pottery, cave walls, carvings, and other discovered reports turned into fabricated explanations.

However, documented history proved they had existed with people.

Thou didst divide the sea by thy strength: thou brakest the heads of the dragons in the waters. Thou brakest the heads of leviathan in pieces, and gavest him to be meat to the people inhabiting the wilderness.

– Psalm 74:13-14

In that day the LORD with his sore and great and strong sword shall punish leviathan the piercing serpent, even leviathan that crooked serpent; and he shall slay the dragon that is in the sea.

– Isaiah 27:1

The Revelation Happened

Behold now behemoth, which I made with thee; he eateth grass as an ox. Lo now, his strength is in his loins, and his force is in the navel of his belly. He moveth his tail like a cedar: the sinews of his stones are wrapped together. His bones are as strong pieces of brass; his bones are like bars of iron.
He is the chief of the ways of God: he that made him can make his sword to approach unto him. Surely the mountains bring him forth food, where all the beasts of the field play.
He lieth under the shady trees, in the covert of the reed, and fens. The shady trees cover him with their shadow; the willows of the brook compass him about. Behold, he drinketh up a river, and hasteth not: he trusteth that he can draw up Jordan into his mouth. He taketh it with his eyes: his nose pierceth through snares.
(God later describes a "fire" sneezing dragon).

– *Job 40:15-24*

What animal other than a behemoth dinosaur can feed from the tops of mountains, have a tail as large as a cedar tree, or can drink up a river? History has documented hundreds if not thousands of enormous dragons and reptiles in the recent past. A few more examples we can research:

Herodotus: Was a Greek historian during the fifth century BC. During a trip to Buto, Arabia, he discovered spines and bones of serpents, similar to a water snake but with wings similar to a bat.

Alexander the Great: Invaded India in 330 BC and reported that people worshiped a huge hissing dragon in a cave. The king of India kept serpents 120–210 feet long. Later, Greek rulers brought back live dragons from Ethiopia.

Morvidus: King of the Britons from 341-336 BC. After a gigantic dragon appeared from the Irish Sea and began devouring the citizens, Morvidus tried to protect his people. He attempted to kill the dragon, but the dragon swallowed him alive instead.

Marco Polo: He traveled and explored much of Asia in the thirteenth century, documenting the customs, plants, and animals in the area. Near a province named Karajan, he described finding gigantic snakes and serpents, fifty feet long with a hundred-inch circumference. He also found dragons and described them as follows:

> *"At the fore part, near the head, they have two short legs, each with three claws, as well as eyes larger than a loaf and very glaring. The jaws are wide enough to swallow a man, the teeth are large and sharp, and their whole appearance is so formidable that neither man, nor any kind of animal can approach them without terror."* [2]

Recently discovered dragon/dinosaur fossils contained tissues and blood in them, which obviously could not have survived millions of years. Scientists try to get us to believe an ancient asteroid killed off the dragons or dinosaurs, when recent changes in environment and humans were the culprit.

Reptiles will keep growing from birth until death. Before the flood and shortly thereafter, people and animals lived much longer, as long as hundreds of years. After the flood, it's possible the atmospheric pressure declined on our earth, eventually leaving far less oxygen for the enormous creatures to breathe.

In addition, life spans are much shorter now, at least compared to life spans post flood, according to Jewish genealogy or ancient Sumerian texts.

We still have lizards or dragons, just not the size that once roamed our earth. Since these enormous beasts terrified people, villagers engaged warriors to destroy them. Either lack of air pressure or man or both caused their destruction.

Cartoonists have drawn an overloaded Noah's ark stuffed with animals such as giraffes and dinosaurs sticking their heads out of the ark. Their mockery implies gigantic animals could in no way fit on the ark.

What the cartoonists and others don't realize is that Noah brought baby or juvenile land and fowl animals on the ark. They would eat less, produce less waste, and be easier to care for. It was also necessary to bring the younger animals so they would have more time to begin the breeds to the variety we observe today.

Until a few hundred years ago, many scientists believed a flood formed the geological layers (or strata) of our earth because that is what the evidence showed. This changed after a self-trained Scottish scientist named James Hutton studied a small area of land. He noticed a slow change from erosion—formed layers of earth and theorized it would take millions of years to create the earth's strata.

Therefore, he concluded, it wasn't catastrophic geological changes or flood, but worldwide slow erosion, and the lower layers were the oldest by millions, if not billions, of years. From this, he developed a uniformitarianism (slow change) theory (instead of catastrophic) and published his works in volumes titled—*Theory of the Earth.*

Around the same time, a self-educated scientist named William Smith discovered from a coal mine he worked in that sometimes certain fossils seemed aligned in particular strata. It was from this discovery that he developed the first geological map.

Thereafter, presuming if someone wanted to know which fossil was older; the person could observe a located layer of earth. In obvious circular reasoning, if someone wanted to know how old a layer of earth was, the person could observe the fossil type located therein.

In their apparent zeal to disprove God and promote a billion-year-plus geological evolution, no one saw the obvious *unscientific* method of circular reasoning taken in their theories, which students still learn today as fact.

In the twentieth century, two new measurements entered the scientific scene to measure the age of organisms and rocks: *Carbon 14 dating* and *radioactive decay*. Scientists assumed carbon and radioactive decay were stable and had not changed over thousands, even millions of years.

Evolutionary scientists overlook the errors of these tools—their assumptions. The most they know is these decay rates were stable only from their discovery a few decades ago, but then assuming this same decay rate of an object back to its beginning. If a person already "knows" the answer is millions of years, then on the other side of the equation it is possible to manipulate the formulas to achieve that answer.

To determine the decay rates, scientists created an assumption about how much carbon and radioactivity was available before decay to measure thousands of years for carbon or eons for radioactivity, and the decay rates were constant.

Alas, no scientist was available thousands or millions of years ago to prove when things began to decay. No one existed through the eons of years to determine the constancy of decay. All the scientist can do is look at what the decay and ratio is today and then create the formulas to equal the assumption "they already know".

As time goes forward, these measuring-tool assumptions will change as we learn how historical universal forces (from volcano eruptions to sun bursts of radiation) skewed decay rates and ratios.

We are seeing how Mystery Babylon's deception has infiltrated everything. But how did it begin? It began when we were first deceived. Lucifer fooled us into believing we could exist without having God intercourse His Spirit into ours.

We pulled our plug on the light of God (turned away), our knowledge of God darkened, and we learned an uncreated God never existed. We don't emit the light of God now, but we did before our fall, and thankfully, His Spirit can restore us into His light again.

For ye were sometimes darkness, but now are ye light in the Lord: walk as children of light.

- Ephesians 5:8

As taught by religious tradition, this describes a person before and after their conversion into Jesus. But when Jesus baptizes us, it expands the words of the Bible into the spirit world and we can walk as children of light, knowing the kingdom of God once again.

Many scientists and religious leaders are clueless about their need for the Holy Spirit to reveal the light and depths of God and the Bible. Hopefully, this book can reveal the darkness they are wandering in throughout their lives.

But the natural man receiveth not the things of the Spirit of God: for they are foolishness unto him: neither can he know them, because they are spiritually discerned.

- 1 Corinthians 2:14

Don Nordstrom

What Are Babylonian Inspired Religions?

And the woman was arrayed in purple and scarlet colour, and decked with gold and precious stones and pearls, having a golden cup in her hand full of abominations and filthiness of her fornication: And upon her forehead was a name written, MYSTERY, BABYLON THE GREAT, THE MOTHER OF HARLOTS AND ABOMINATIONS OF THE EARTH.

– **Revelation 17:4–5**

For the mystery of iniquity doth already work: only he who now letteth will let, until he be taken out of the way.

– **2 Thessalonians 2:7**

As we will later show, the temple leaders committed spiritual adultery, and brought Babylon adornments and idol worship (abominations) into the temple. She had become Mystery Babylon.

When the Roman Catholic religion formed, they brought her adornments and idol abominations into their worship, which later passed into her organized religious denominations.

God gave biblical prophets pre-access to His kingdom. They prophesied current and future events for the Jewish people. These prophets warned the Jews what would happen by disrespecting the covenant blessings and protection from God.

The apostle John received special access to the spiritual kingdom in Revelation. God showed him why the judgment came in his time.

The idol-god worshiping Babylonian religions, and how they dispersed worldwide, fill book shelves in libraries. These descendants of Satan inspired religions had spread into certain seven churches. John learns through Revelation what happens to these churches if they continue in their practices, which they will soon witness the judgment upon Jerusalem and the Mystery Babylon worshipers.

What we are pointing out here is Mystery Babylon as the "mother of harlots and of the abominations of the earth". Mystery Babylon is not the kingdom of Babylon- it is her adulterous belief systems, which the world and false Jewish leaders adopted into their temples. This would be similar if our spouse spitefully and continuously committed adultery in our face. How long could we put up with it?

The mystery is iniquity. Therefore, we have the iniquities of Babylon; we need to find out what iniquity means and what it is has to do with Babylon.

The iniquity or mystery of Babylon is any belief that twists or goes against the will or Word of the uncreated God. The mother of harlots (the pagan Queen of Heaven) overtook Jerusalem as the temple blended the Mosaic law with the adopted pagan myths of Babylon.

Previously in history, Babylonians had conquered and kidnapped the Jews, destroying their temple and Jerusalem, enslaving them to Babylon and its pagan idol worship.

After the Persian king, Cyrus II, defeated Babylon in 538 BC, he freed the Jews, many who then began their slow return to Jerusalem, bringing the knowledge of Babylon's idol worship with them.

After they rebuilt their temple and Jerusalem, they later brought in Babylon's abominations into their temple.

Iniquity had started the belief systems of Mystery Babylon, where people intentionally turned away from God to create and worship their created idols as gods.

There were gods, goddesses, and sibyls created from the Satan inspired imaginations of people. Now, instead of God, deceptive mystic powers from the mythic gods and nature created everything.

Goddesses became elevated to the *Queen of Heaven*, and her name changed with her nature and character as kingdoms overtook other kingdoms and they adopted their gods as their own.

The gods and goddess myths drew the Jews away from God to worship them.

The children gather wood, and the fathers kindle the fire, and the women knead their dough, to make cakes to the queen of heaven, and to pour out drink offerings unto other gods, that they may provoke me to anger.

– Jeremiah 7:18

This pagan idol god worship started after the (Noah) flood occurred, when a mighty hunter named Nimrod rose as a Satan inspired god and ruler. He was the son of Cush, who was the great-grandson of Noah. Nimrod had enslaved children to build a tower to heaven.

When Lucifer fell from Eden and God's world, with his fallen angels and with our fallen spirits, his name changed to Satan. He now rules our world through Mystic Babylon, while developing his seed or followers.

Satan is angry at his quarantine with us on earth and wants to ascend back into heaven. It has always been Satan's motive to overtake God, deceive, rule over people, and destroy the works of God.

For thou hast said in thine heart, I will ascend into heaven, I will exalt my throne above the stars of God: I will sit also upon the mount of the congregation, in the sides of the north: I will ascend above the heights of the clouds; I will be like the most High.

- Isaiah 14:13-14

Nimrod becomes a seed in Satan's plan to build a tower, to ascend back to heaven and finish the destruction Lucifer started. As Nimrod continued following the lead of Satan, he built kingdoms and ruled over his people.

He was a mighty hunter before the LORD: wherefore it is said, Even as Nimrod the mighty hunter before the LORD. And the beginning of his kingdom was Babel, and Erech, and Accad, and Calneh, in the land of Shinar.

- Genesis 10:9-10

And the whole earth was of one language, and of one speech. And it came to pass, as they journeyed from the east, that they found a plain in the land of Shinar; and they dwelt there.

– Genesis 11:1-2

Shinar was a fruitful area full of vegetation and animals. The fear of man was in the animals, so it is doubtful the animals were attacking people.

This implies Nimrod was a trophy hunter and killed for sport "before the Lord" (or in His face), again under Satan to kill and show spite for what God had created.

And they said one to another, Go to, let us make brick, and burn them thoroughly. And they had brick for stone, and slime had they for morter.
And they said, Go to, let us build us a city and a tower, whose top may reach unto heaven; and let us make us a name, lest we be scattered abroad upon the face of the whole earth.

– Genesis 11:3-4

This shows the start of turning away from the will of God, as they were to scatter worldwide, but stayed in one place, with one motive.

The slime for mortar was a type of tar, as archaeologists discovered tiles and bricks mortared with bitumen tar in Babylon, Iraq. According to the Jewish historian Josephus, it would provide waterproofing for the tower in case God brought another flood.

It seems probable, Nimrod enslaved children because the adults still knew the teachings of the true God from their fathers, and he wanted to rule over them as their god. Adults also probably wanted no part in working with tar. God told the descendants of Noah to scatter and populate the earth, but Nimrod goes against God; they became one people against God and settled in Shinar to build a tower for Satan.

And the Lord came down to see the city and the tower, which the children of men builded. And the Lord said, Behold, the people is one, and they have all one language; and this they begin to do: and now nothing will be restrained from them, which they have imagined to do.

Go to, let us go down, and there confound their language, that they may not understand one another's speech. So the Lord scattered them abroad from thence upon the face of all the earth: and they left off to build the city.

Therefore is the name of it called Babel; because the Lord did there confound the language of all the earth: and from thence did the Lord scatter them abroad upon the face of all the earth.

- Genesis 11:5-9

The reason for the tower was to return to heaven with Satan, since God's kingdom had sat above the spiritual earth or on the holy mountain of God (Ezekiel 28:14).

There was one language or purpose: to build the tower and kingdoms in opposition to God. God confounds their language so they could not accomplish their purpose. The children left to follow God's original plan to populate the earth, which was better than enslavement under Nimrod.

The tower turned into Satan's first earthly base of operation, and demonic worship started where his followers learned that forces from the sun, moon, stars, and planets controlled the earth and their lives.

As knowledge spread into "The Builders", they developed the stonemason tools and technologies needed to build temples and idols, and this knowledge passed on to other kingdoms.

Then What Happened?

Pagans learned the sun caused vegetation to grow, then worshiped its power. The moon and stars comforted them in their fear of darkness. The constellation bodies appeared to move, causing the change of seasons.

These astral powers became gods and goddesses and idols to worship, and these deceptions spread into secret societies.

This mystic knowledge from Babylon later passed down through a group called the Craft, or Freemasons, who placed their insignia on towering buildings, monuments, and obelisks in memoriam of once powerful people.

Other branches included the Odd Fellows, the Bohemian Club, OTO, fraternal Skull and Bones, among others. Their symbolism is everywhere in plain sight.

Many powerful people and presidents of the United States were Masons or involved with other secret societies.

Most people do not know that the Masons have their own Constitution (see Anderson's Constitution of 1723), and if push came to shove, which Constitution would the government follow? Which *Lord* is their Master?

Mystery schools became available, where people trained in the secret arts. Innumerable people daily believe the zodiac horoscope has power over their lives. We also worship movie, sports, and rock "stars".

Occultist secret societies use the belief systems from Babylon. They learn to twist the Christian God into being the one to blame for the pain and misery we suffer throughout our lives. They need to destroy Christianity because Christians stole their "secrets" and created their false god, Jesus. The mystic beliefs change one letter in the word *Son* to *sun* and worship the sun.

The secret teaches that Satan will soon take over and liberate everyone from a belief in God. Through political science, politicians learn from ancient Greeks and philosophers how to bring all people under the control of Mystic Babylon, disguised as socialism. Once all governments control our lives under socialism is when Satan will rear his head as ruler of the world.

Why does the back of our dollar bill have a "seal" with an opened pyramid, Roman numerals etched in the base, a watching eye with a glorified sun behind? Why are the words in Latin, the language of Rome? We will soon find out.

How can we change government for the better when we gave them a conflict of interest in power over our lives by controlling our education, retirement, medical care, and so forth? Our Founding Fathers would start an insurrection from their graves if they knew we allowed our government to fund even one social program. The plan is to bring people under the rule of social programs. And again, who would rule once governments are under one ideal of socialist democracy?

Socialist democracy dupes many people into believing it is the ideal government to control all aspects of our lives. Travel to any country controlled in a non-parliamentary socialist democracy, and we discover the extreme poverty, the gang-ruled streets, and people fleeing to find freedom elsewhere.

During the old time, in the old world (spiritual realm), Lucifer, clothed in jewels, walked among the fiery (sparkling) stones in Eden. He reflected the awesome glory of God and His kingdom.

> *Thou hast been in Eden the garden of God; every precious stone was thy covering, the sardius, topaz, and the diamond, the beryl, the onyx, and the jasper, the sapphire, the emerald, and the carbuncle, and gold: the workmanship of thy tabrets and of thy pipes was prepared in thee in the day that thou wast created.*
>
> *Thou art the anointed cherub that covereth; and I have set thee so: thou wast upon the holy mountain of God; thou hast walked up and down in the midst of the stones of fire. Thou wast perfect in thy ways from the day that thou wast created, till iniquity was found in thee.*
>
> – Ezekiel 28:13–15

Now we know why we believe gold and jewels seem valuable. Royals wear crowns embedded with gems that reflect light and their glory. The crowns appear with "rays" to portray the symbolic power of the sun shining upon their heads. We wear fiery jewelry to reflect light and bring attention to ourselves.

Iniquity first came from Lucifer and is in Mystery Babylon as Satan. He is deceiving people away from God's salvation plan by creating religious belief systems. When we allow them to control our lives, it gives them power over us.

Knowing or not, we use symbols inspired by Babylon in branding objects we create.

We:

-drive vehicles named Taurus, Aries, Ram, Mercury, and Saturn.

-watch a TV station with a watching eye.

-admire a smiley face on a sun.

-eat at the golden arches or drink coffee at a shop that uses a logo of a woman with a crown and star.

-snack on Mars and Milky Way candy bars.

-name cities Phoenix, Oracle, the "city of angels" Los Angeles, or a first name of a Saint (e.g., St. Louis, etc.).

-construct towering buildings, revel in the Statue of Liberty, devise war plans at a Pentagon shaped building, marvel at the Washington Monument obelisk and other monuments, and nothing is wrong with a bull statue near Wall Street in New York? (Pagans drank blood from strangled bulls in their temples).

Do we now have any doubt why an Egyptian obelisk brought to Rome by the emperor Caligula stands in the courtyard of the Vatican?

Media and entertainment display the Catholic Church as the only church. Our Catholic leaders or politicians still recognize the pope as the religious authority over the world.

Our judges wear black robes and pass judgment on us from their "chambers" in buildings with statues and carvings of idols.

We've allowed Babylonian beliefs into our churches, not to honor God but to bring honor to Mystery Babylon. Anyone who takes a moment to look around will see how she has subliminally infiltrated her control into our lives.

How Do Religions Honor Mystery Babylon?

Ash Wednesday: Pope Gregory brought this pagan tradition into the Roman religion. It symbolized a mark to begin a forty-day fast during pagan Lent.

Some claim the rubbing of black ash on the forehead or hand stems from the mark of the beast in Revelation. However, it is a sign of disobedience. The mark occurs despite Jesus telling us not to make any external expression if we fast, and to wash our face!

> *But thou, when thou fastest, anoint thine head, and wash thy face;*
> *That thou appear not unto men to fast,*
> *but unto thy Father which is in secret: and thy Father, which seeth in secret, shall reward thee openly.*
>
> *– Matthew 6:17–18*

Lent: This entanglement is in several false doctrines and beliefs. None of the doctrines of Lent is in the Bible, nor did Jesus command them from us. The main false doctrine is that since Jesus fasted for forty days in the desert, then we should too.

The basis of Lent allegedly comes from an ancient god named Tammuz (later, Osiris of Egyptian and Adonis of Greek mythology).

Tammuz was a god of agriculture who died, and the queen of heaven, Ishtar, mourned his death in the early spring for forty days until he came back to life again. The disobedient Jews also took part in mourning.

Then he brought me to the door of the gate of the LORD's house which was toward the north; and, behold, there sat women weeping for Tammuz.

- Ezekiel 8:14

This pagan religion also grew into a mother-child cult, duplicated in almost every pagan mythology as a female goddess, including Mary as the "Mother of God" in the Roman Catholic Church.

Good Friday and Easter: Any child can do the math without a seminary degree and figure out if Jesus's burial was for three days and three nights—something is amiss.

For as Jonas was three days and three nights in the whale's belly; so shall the Son of man be three days and three nights in the heart of the earth.

- Matthew 12:40

If the crucifixion of Jesus was on a Friday, then His burial was only two days and nights.

First, Good Friday and Easter have nothing to do with the crucifixion of Jesus or His resurrection. They have everything to do with the pagan celebration of the vernal equinox, when the sun crosses the equator and day and night are equal lengths of time. Pagans began their festivities of fertility on the first day of spring as the sun brought its power to birth crops in the fields.

Once again, we have to look back to Constantine to find out how Easter started. He ordered Easter (not the resurrection of Jesus) as the first Sunday after the first full moon after the spring equinox.

So why did the Roman false church select Good Friday and Easter?

Venus is the Roman name for the Greek goddess Aphrodite, and Romans worshiped her on Friday. In Greek mythology, she either turned into a fish or disguised herself as a fish to escape a monster. In either case, the story developed within the constellation Pisces (zodiac sign of the fish). The spring equinox occurs in the constellation Pisces.

After the death of Jesus, we were in the mystic astrological sign of the fish, Pisces. Organized religion adopted this symbol of a fish, and the pagan Roman religion instructs their unknowing followers to eat fish on Friday to honor Venus.

During the First Council of Nicene, Constantine's interest was harmonizing the different religious beliefs within his empire.

He, along with the Roman Empire, worshiped the sun god, Sol, on Sunday, including other gods throughout the week. The spring ritual rites of worship were like the renewal of life. It only made sense to Constantine to worship these rites along with the crucifixion and resurrection of Jesus from Friday to Sunday. But, to count for three days and nights, Jesus had to be in the tomb before Thursday evening.

The Bible says the Jews wanted Him buried before the Sabbath, which would have occurred on a Saturday. God had declared Saturday–Sabbath not as a day of worship, but as a day of rest or *no work* for His people.

But there were other Sabbath days or no-work days (holy convocations) His people were to honor. These Sabbaths were the feasts of the Lord.

> *These are the feasts of the* LORD, *even holy convocations, which ye shall proclaim in their seasons. In the fourteenth day of the first month at even is the* LORD's *passover. And on the fifteenth day of the same month is the feast of unleavened bread unto the* LORD: *seven days ye must eat unleavened bread. In the first day ye shall have an holy convocation: ye shall do no servile work therein.*
>
> **- Leviticus 23:4-7**

> *Speak unto the children of Israel, saying, In the seventh month, in the first day of the month, shall ye have a sabbath, a memorial of blowing of trumpets, an holy convocation. Ye shall do no servile work therein: but ye shall offer an offering made by fire unto the Lord.*
>
> **- Leviticus 23:24-25**

Verse 5, in the previous first example, says Passover occurs on the evening of the fourteenth day of the *first* month. The next day starts the Feast of Unleavened Bread, beginning on the fifteenth, and His people were to do no work on this holy convocation sabbath day.

We need to clear this up since Passover and the crucifixion did not happen in our first month, January. The Jews used a lunar calendar that differed from the Roman calendar. *Nisan* was the Jewish first month and occurred on the Roman calendar in March.

The day after Passover was a sabbath day of no work on the feast of Unleavened Bread. The crucifixion of Jesus occurred on Passover, and the Jews wanted Jesus off the cross before this

Sabbath feast of unleavened bread started, and not because of the Saturday Sabbath.

Since the Jews started their day in the evening, this means their Passover started on Passover evening. The crucifixion took place the following morning (still Passover) and placed Him in the tomb before their next evening-day, which was the start of the unleavened bread sabbath. Therefore, Jesus was in the tomb on *their* Passover, their feast of bread sabbath, and the Saturday Sabbath. Two eyewitnesses also indirectly verified Jesus's crucifixion happened three days prior to Sunday.

Now upon the first day of the week, very early in the morning, they came unto the sepulchre [tomb], bringing the spices which they had prepared, and certain others with them. And they found the stone rolled away from the sepulchre. And they entered in, and found not the body of the Lord Jesus.

– Luke 24:1–3

And, behold, two of them went that same day to a village called Emmaus, which was from Jerusalem about threescore furlongs. And they talked together of all these things which had happened. And it came to pass, that, while they communed together and reasoned, Jesus himself drew near, and went with them. But their eyes were holden that they should not know him.

– Luke 24:13–16

And he said unto them, What things? And they said unto him, Concerning Jesus of Nazareth, which was a prophet mighty in deed and word before God and all the people:

And how the chief priests and our rulers delivered him to be condemned to death, and have crucified him.

But we trusted that it had been he which should have redeemed Israel: and beside all this, <u>to day is the third day since these things were done</u>. (underline added)

- Luke 24:19-21

They said it was the third day *since*, or after, the crucifixion. Therefore, the crucifixion most likely occurred on Thursday, as Friday would be the first day *since* the crucifixion, Saturday the second day, and Sunday the third day.

The Jews celebrated their Passover with the roasting and eating of a lamb. Jesus' shed blood transformed Him from the Passover lamb.

Jesus and the disciples told no one to celebrate His resurrection on Sunday. What Jesus did during His last supper with His disciples at Passover was change the eating of a lamb to a communion. Our communion remembers Jesus through the breaking (eating) of bread (His body) and drinking of wine (His shed blood for us).

This is what Jesus instructed us to do at our supper: to break bread and drink wine, remembering what He did for us on the cross. Religions have distorted this personal communion of remembrance, as only they can perform Communion in their church.

Many people and families pray at suppertime, eating bread and some drinking wine (or fruit of the vine), but do we remember the death and resurrection of Jesus?

We are *not* to embrace Roman pagan rites or Mystery Babylon to worship the sunrise on Easter or introduce our children to deceptions of pagan rites of fertility with an Easter Bunny and decorated eggs.

Advent and Christmas: These religious rites involve the Roman gods Saturn and Mithras. Advent in religions disguises this by honoring anticipation toward Christmas, or the Catholic *Christ Mass.*

The Romans celebrated advent as Saturnalia in anticipating the crowning of the king of Saturnalia. It included the Winter Solstice—when the *sun* "was born" and began its route north to warm the Roman Empire. Saturnalia ran from December 17 through the 30th on the Roman calendar. It started with a sacrifice at the temple of Saturn.

Mithra's was a sun god from Persia that the Roman military adopted during their wars, and worshiped as being born on December 25th, as their Sun god. To get pagans into the Roman church, they quickly tied the birth of God's Son to the birth of a Sun god. A Mithra's statue, in fact, stands in the Vatican library.

Not only is the worship of Saturnalia and Mithras absurd, but so is Christmas as the birthday of Jesus on December 25. Jews and early Christians never celebrated their own birthdays or for anyone else. Only pagan royalty celebrated birthdays. The Jews considered their birthdays as cursed, most likely from all the endless suffering endured from their unfaithfulness towards God during their lives.

No one knows for sure when Jesus was born, but it was not in the middle of winter, as shepherds were still in the fields at night with their sheep. There would have been no reason to have sheep out at night in the middle of winter. In addition, there was a Roman census happening (Joseph and Mary went to Bethlehem for this), which would not have occurred in the winter.

Romans celebrated Saturnalia as "crazy days". After the sacrifice to Saturn, there was a grand banquet, a king of Saturnalia crowned, gifts exchanged, gambling, plenty of drinking and revelries, and masters served their servants (time off work). They also closed public offices and schools.

Christ Mass (Christmas) has nothing to do with the birth of Jesus. It is from the revived Roman Empire, disguised as the Roman Catholic Church, celebrating an advent of the King of Saturnalia, the worship of Saturn and Mithras.

Should we deceive our children by introducing them to a perverted Santa who tells children to sit on his lap and they will get a toy? Do we need a stalking terrorist who frightens children with a ritual song?

> *You better watch out,*
> *you better not cry,*
> *you better not pout…*
> *Santa Claus is coming to town.*
> *He sees you when you're sleeping,*
> *he knows when you're awake,*
> *he knows if you've been bad or good,*
> *so be good for goodness' sake.*

Children connect a fearful Santa with Jesus, whom they should not fear. We ingrain this deception in them until they can make the disconnect, and we need to stop lying to our children.

Once we wake up from our deceptions and understand what is happening, we will see Mystery Babylon alive and well in our churches and controlling our lives. God warned seven churches two thousand years ago, and we need to heed His warning today.

When John receives the revelation of Mystery Babylon, God tells us to get out.

And I heard another voice from heaven, saying, Come out of her, my people, that ye be not partakers of her sins, and that ye receive not of her plagues. For her sins have reached unto heaven, and God hath remembered her iniquities.

— Revelation 18:4–5

How Can We Know What the True Church Is?

He [Jesus] saith unto them, But whom say ye that I am? And Simon Peter answered and said, Thou art the Christ, the Son of the living God.

And Jesus answered and said unto him, Blessed art thou, Simon Barjona [son of Jona]: for flesh and blood hath not revealed it unto thee, but my Father, which is in heaven.

And I say also unto thee, That thou art Peter, and upon this rock I will build my church; and the gates of hell shall not prevail against it. [added by author]

– **Matthew 16:15-18**

These are the verses that the false church uses to claim the apostle Peter was the first pope and built their Roman religion upon him.

But once again, they are distorting what the Word is saying

It doesn't say Jesus will build His church on Peter but upon "this rock". What is "this rock"? Jesus said that flesh and blood had not revealed to Simon who Jesus was but the Father in heaven. Simon became a rock (Peter) with his revelation from God—*not* through a person or religion, only from the Father revealing Jesus to Peter.

If the Father reveals Jesus to us, wouldn't we become a rock in our spirit? We are the true church; whom the Father reveals Jesus to will become a rock, and the gates of hell will not prevail against it or us.

There is one body, and one Spirit, even as ye are called in one hope of your calling; One Lord, one faith, one baptism, One God and Father of all, who is above all, and through all, and in you all.

- Ephesians 4:4-6

It is the calling of the Holy Spirit from God that reveals Jesus to us. This is how the NT church could stand up to the temple with false leaders and torturers, knowing it was possible they could execute them.

Believing can be difficult because of our exposure to the deceptive mystical practices that lead us away from the uncreated Jesus. But Jesus did not leave us to fend for ourselves in the wilderness. Remember, John the Baptist said Jesus would baptize a believer with the Holy Spirit *and* with fire.

God, in the Old Testament, proved beyond doubt that no matter what He did, our evil nature could not consistently love or exist with Him. We'd always turn away from our cure of eternal death into destruction. The false Jewish leaders denied Jesus and His warnings and stuck with their religious temple doctrines.

Jesus warned of the coming destruction of their temple:

And as he went out of the temple, one of his disciples saith unto him, Master, see what manner of stones and what buildings are here!
And Jesus answering said unto him, Seest thou these great buildings? there shall not be left one stone upon another, that shall not be thrown down.

- Mark 13:1-2

This occurred during the Jewish Wars in AD 66–70, and the end of the OT temple age. With the impending destruction of Jerusalem, the temple, and countless Jews starved to death, crucified, enslaved to the Romans, or deported—the Spirit-baptized church stood as beacons in the world for God's kingdom.

The false Jews denied Jesus was their savior—promised from the OT. They did not believe His Spirit kingdom could live within us, and then we would exist in peace with God.

The baptism of fire in the apostles gave them undying courage. He instilled different tongues in them, along with other gifts, enabling their teaching and serving different dialects in the empire (Acts 2).

The apostles now spoke with courage in front of the Jewish leaders and people and Roman leaders—teaching that they could receive the baptism through the risen Jesus.

We, too, can have the Holy Spirit and the fire (courage and spiritual gifts). It is available to everyone who believes.

Then said Jesus to them again, Peace be unto you: as my Father hath sent me, even so send I you. And when he had said this, he breathed on [the apostles], and saith unto them, Receive ye the Holy Ghost.

- John 20:21-22

And when the day of Pentecost was fully come, they were all with one accord in one place.

And suddenly there came a sound from heaven as of a rushing mighty wind, and it filled all the house where they were sitting. And there appeared unto them cloven tongues like as of fire, and it sat upon each of them.

And they were all filled with the Holy Ghost, and began to speak with other tongues, as the Spirit gave them utterance.

– Acts 2:1–4

Jesus said unto her, I am the resurrection, and the life: he that believeth in me, though he were dead, yet shall he live: And whosoever liveth and believeth in me shall never die. Believest thou this?

– John 11:25–27

Do we believe this? We need to ask the Father to reveal Jesus to us. We need to make a quality decision; either He raised Jesus from the dead, Jesus came to save us from our eternal disease so we can return to Him and live forever, or He didn't.

The only way we can know God is to repent and have His spirit baptized into us with His fire. Pray for His spirit-baptism now.

Jesus answered and said unto him, If a man love me, he will keep my words: and my Father will love him, and we will come unto him, and make our abode with him.

– John 14:23

The Roman Empire and the Jewish Population

Before we delve into Revelation, we need to look deeper into some history of the Jews up to our current time.

During the early first century AD, there was unrest in the temple with the Jewish leaders; the Scribes and Pharisees, the Sadducees, and the Sanhedrin council, who were arguing over which doctrines and laws to keep and enslave their followers. Then the Zealots brought their aggression against the Romans into the temple with the leaders.

As this and developing troubles with the Romans and others came about, the Jewish leaders formed the militant Judean Free Government. Seven priests converted to generals and led the Jews to defend the hostilities brought upon the temple, Jerusalem, and other towns and villages.

At first, the generals were successful at keeping their attackers at bay, stopping a few assaults. But, within three-and-one-half years, the armies under Rome would overtake Israel, the temple, and Jerusalem.

There is little doubt the Romans rank at the top of ruthless empires. They enacted the worse punishments and tortures imaginable and slaughtered the condemned through crucifixion. Victims often suffered days of excruciating pain and then slow asphyxiation hanging from a cross until dead.

When God poked the essence of His being into our world to form Jesus, He said little of the cruelty of the Roman Empire and much about the Jewish temple's false religious leaders. Jesus saw them as eviler.

> *But woe unto you, scribes and Pharisees, hypocrites! For ye shut up the kingdom of heaven against men: for ye neither go in yourselves, neither suffer ye them that are entering to go in.*
>
> *Woe unto you, scribes and Pharisees, hypocrites! For ye devour widows' houses,*
>
> *and for a pretence make long prayer: therefore ye shall receive the greater damnation.*
>
> *– Matthew 23:13-14*

It is interesting to note that Augustus Caesar was the Roman emperor when Jesus came into our world. Augustus was the adopted son of Julius, who previously rose to the position of a god (Caesar). Therefore, Augustus took on the additional title, the *son of god*. Jesus' disciples, demons, and others would later identify Jesus as the true Son of God. This is one reason the Romans hated the followers of Jesus.

The Roman government was always in flux; however, their military was quite capable of conquering foreign countries and adopting their gods in with their own. Augustus built palaces and restored temples for each of the gods to give citizens a secure place for their pagan worship.

Since there were plentiful gods to worship, with Caesars as the top gods to give tribute to, the Romans (at first) cared little for the monotheistic (one God) the enslaved Jews worshiped.

But this would eventually change when the apostles and their Spirit-baptized converts would claim Jesus as their God, only to endure centuries of persecution before the Romans would accept religious Christianity as an additional religion under their terms.

The Roman Empire existed under a class system where the Roman elite enjoyed more liberties, wealth, and choice than the bottom class or slaves. There were censuses conducted to establish who and how many people were under which class. In turn, a tax system determined what each person's obligation was to pay taxes for the roads and the relative peace, religious security, and enjoyment of their liberties, if any.

(Is it a coincidence the Romans had their roads built just before the apostles would use them to spread the good news of the risen Jesus to the world?)

The Jews, at first, considered payment of tribute to the Caesars a sin, and to make matters worse, the Jews considered the Jewish tax collector a traitor and hated as the worst of all sinners.

The Roman tax on the Jews was arbitrary; however, the collectors would often extort far more tax than what was due and pocket the excess.

In addition, there was the temple tax to pay to the temple leaders for their lavish lifestyles and for maintenance of the temple. And instead of the temple helping the poor with their needs or wants, Jesus pointed out; they would instead take their last two cents:

And there came a certain poor widow, and she threw in two mites, which make a farthing. And he called unto him his disciples, and saith unto them,

Verily I say unto you, That this poor widow hath cast more in, than all they which have cast into the treasury: For all they did cast in of their abundance; but she of her want did cast in all that she had, even all her living.

– *Mark 12:42-44*

Roman soldiers roamed among the Jews, and with any revolt or disrespect towards Rome, the soldiers immediately met them with barbed lashes, imprisonment, or crucifixion. There were always crucifixions taking place in plain sight on the hill to keep the Jews intimidated.

Because of the corrupt and stifling taxes, the cruelty of the Roman soldiers, and disagreement with the temple leaders, a group of Zealot Jews rose against the temple leaders and the Roman military.

There were many Zealot factions in the empire that attacked the military camps, their ships, and supply lines. From a Roman or outsider's viewpoint, it is because of the Zealots that the torture and killing of Jews occurred. The Zealots would later attack their own temple and the villages throughout their land, those who would not join their forces.

After the wars of AD 66–70 and a following revolt at Masada in AD 70–74, there was a final Jewish revolt.

Remnant Jews had partially rebuilt the temple and Jerusalem, and temporarily took control for this revolt period of about three and one-half years (AD 132–135) during Emperor Hadrian's rule.

Hadrian had erected a statue of Jupiter in the temple, which started the revolt. After the slaughter of thousands of more Jews during this last revolt, and many enslaved or deported, Hadrian removed any reference to the Jews and Israel, and changed the name of their land to Palestine.

Except for a brief period of Persian (Iranian) control, the Roman Empire ruled over the land until about AD 638. A new antichrist religion, started by Muhammad, erupted out of Arabia.

After Muhammad's death, a Muslim named Ali caused a split with the followers into two factions. Despite continuous infighting (which still goes on today), they united under Islam. The militant side took over Jerusalem, and the Islamic religion spread throughout the empire.

Muhammad had adopted the Mesopotamian moon god, Sîn (the greatest of all gods), which the Arabs called Allah. A crescent moon emblem went with this god, and Islam used it as a banner in their religion.

The conquering Islamic religion somewhat tolerated the Jews and Gentiles as long as they either converted to Islam or paid a tax (Jizya). Many Jews and Christians fled to other countries.

In about AD 1100, the Roman Catholic religion started the Crusades to take back Jerusalem, which resulted in the slaughter of thousands of Muslims and Jews.

The Muslim's and the Catholic's battled back and forth for control. This left the land in ruins, and only a few people, who lived in extreme poverty, remained. The Ottoman empire would later claim the land until their defeat in World War I.

Around 1880, the Jews began their slow return to Palestine, and their leaders attempted to get other countries to recognize Palestine as Israel once again. The immigration continued, along with more Islamic returning to the area. After World War I, the British and French divided the Middle East under their control.

Despite a few years of relative peace, the Jews and Islamic Arabs constantly fought for land and rights. When Nazi Germany came to power with their well-publicized hatred for Jews, the Arabs were ready to align with Germany. The Nazis then provided the Arabs with weapons, and the skirmishes continued with the Jews until the British came under attack and ended the Arab uprisings.

When World War II began, the Jews aligned with Britain, and many Jews joined the British army. At the end of the war, the newly formed United Nations (UN) set up states of land separating the Palestinian Jews and Arabs.

In 1948, the Jews claimed their sovereignty to the UN as Israel once again, which the UN (under pressure from the USA) reluctantly accepted. The Arabs, and others, rejected their claim, and the Islamic controlled Arab countries proclaimed their right to destroy the Jewish state.

After the Jews declared Israel their home again, hundreds of thousands of Jews emigrated from the surrounding countries and were welcomed. In contrast, when thousands of Arabs wanted to immigrate out of Palestine/Israel into Arab countries, the governments placed them in refugee camps on the borders of Israel, keeping their Palestinian identity even today. These Palestinians, instead of taking their hostilities out on the countries that rejected them, daily attack Israel.

During the Jewish revolt in AD 66, Jerusalem divided into three sects before Rome and other countries could overtake the city. So it is today as Jews, Christians, and Islam occupy the land. Just as hostile countries surrounded Israel, it is the same today.

Despite several weakened peace treaties now in existence, it is still the plan for the Palestinians and Islamic controlled countries to remove Israel from the map. As the major countries of the world align for war with supporting either Israel or the Islamic controlled countries (which are building now), it would seem time is closing in on the last judgment.

This is another prophecy that came true from the OT in the Bible, which states that although God would take Israel away from the Jews and their land deserted, He would restore it for them once again.

> *And say unto them, Thus saith the Lord God; Behold, I will take the children of Israel from among the heathen, whither they be gone, and will gather them on every side, and bring them into their own land:*
> *And I will make them one nation in the land upon the mountains of Israel; and one king shall be king to them all: and they shall be no more two nations, neither shall they be divided into two kingdoms any more at all.* (See also Joel 2)
>
> *– Ezekiel 37:21-22*

Despite many critics stating the Bible is a fable, no one can deny this prophecy fulfillment, which happened in our recent history in 1948.

Despite what deceived religious teachers preach today, there will be no coming seven-year tribulation, a false prophet, or person from the revived Roman Empire as an antichrist.

The great tribulation started when Jesus left in approximately AD 33, the spirit of antichrist appeared after His resurrection, and the false Roman church later began as the revived Roman Empire. This has continued for two thousand years as the great tribulation.

Jesus warned the Jews in person of their coming destruction. But we won't be so lucky when He returns for the last time to destroy our world, and God reveals His spiritual kingdom to all once again.

> *But the day of the Lord will come as a thief in the night; in the which the heavens shall pass away with a great noise,*
> *and the elements shall melt with fervent heat, the earth also and the works that are therein shall be burned up.*
>
> *–2 Peter 3:10*

Don Nordstrom

Preparing to Understand Revelation

Revelation is a unique book in the Bible. It is sort of like a summary of the judgment prophecies from the OT. Most end-time authors are clueless about what the symbols mean and what they are telling us. First-century Jews who had learned the OT would have known the symbols by heart. Revelation uses OT symbolism so the readers or hearers could learn it under the noses of the persecutors or without reprisal from the "beasts".

The symbols are not understandable to us without knowing the OT prophecy, with Jewish and other history of the period. The symbolism proves Revelation is OT prophecy, which describes the destruction of the OT temple age, and restoration of the kingdom of God within us from the Spirit of Jesus.

Nevertheless, many have used assumptions and imaginations, much like the scientists who already know the answers, to write books of our last days from misunderstood scriptures. Bible prophecy and Revelation have little to reveal concerning the final judgment, except it will happen without warning.

What our book teaches is what researchers label *preterist*, as opposed to *futurist*. Preterists teach that by using OT prophecy and recorded history, either most or all of Revelation occurred soon after Jesus's resurrection. In Matthew 24, Jesus personally warned His disciples about the events soon to come and the coming judgment from the Son of Man in their lifetimes.

Futurists claim that Bible prophecy from Daniel, Revelation, Jesus, and His apostles warns what will happen at the end of our current existence. They prey upon the people who want Revelation to unfold during their lives. This twisting of scripture has become a multi-million-dollar book industry, so it is not surprising writers want to profit off of their teachings.

The curious thing is, why would Daniel, Revelation, Jesus, and the apostles teach about the end of our time to the Jews and Gentiles of the day? How could they possibly care about events two thousand-plus years in their future? Wouldn't it be more important to know the horrors soon coming in *their* lifetime and the end of their OT temple system world or age?

None of these matter, as we prove beyond doubt that the preterist view of prophecy and Revelation is by far the most accurate.

There is a style of writing called *chiastic* that can vary from simple to complex. Some people write or speak in this manner, and the Bible has verses showing this style. Some claim the Bible is a *chiasm*.

In chiastic writing, a person scripts a sentence, paragraph, or more and then writes it back in mirrored or reflective form. For example, "When the going gets tough, the tough get going". And as Jesus said:

> *"And he said unto them, The sabbath was made for man, and not man for the sabbath."*
>
> *— Mark 2:27*

A few people view Revelation as a chiasm, and doubt John could write it without this divine inspiration. We won't elaborate on whether the Bible or Revelation is a chiasm because of disagreement with terminology. However, the following will allow a similar overview of Revelation. It shows items in the second part of Revelation reflect from different perspectives in the first half.

a. Introduction (Ch. 1)

b. Seven churches: Jesus contrasts their pagan inclusion with His kingdom (Ch. 2–3)

c. Seven Seals (Ch. 4)

d. The 144,000 and Seven Trumpets (Ch. 7)

e. Two Witnesses (Ch. 11)

f. Woman and the sun (Ch. 12)

g. Dragon (Lucifer) in heaven (Ch. 12)

h. Woman flees to wilderness (Ch. 12)

i. Lucifer as Satan cast out (Ch. 12)

h. Woman flies to wilderness (Ch. 12)

g. Dragon persecutes woman (Ch. 12)

f. Woman's seed keeps God's commandments and testimony of Jesus (Ch. 12)

e. Two Beasts (Ch.13)

d. The 144,000 and Seven Angels (Ch. 14, 15)

c. Seven Bowls (Ch. 15, 16)

b. Seven Angels: contrast Whore vs. New Jerusalem (Ch. 17, 22)

a. Epilog (Ch. 22)

The start of Revelation explains it is a warning to seven churches. Something is about to happen, then we have to find out what the symbols mean, which the book defines itself or in other places in the Bible.

The key symbols, which we show and explain are:

- Judgment is fire, clouds, sun-moon darkening, smoke, stars falling.

Later,

- Rome and the empire are the sea.
- Sea beast is Caesar or Rome.
- Israel is the land or wilderness.
- The earth is Jerusalem or temple under judgment destruction.
- The earth beast is a king appointed by Caesar over the Jews.
- Mystery Babylon is the ancient pagan belief system brought into Jerusalem and the temple.
- The OT temple system ends, and the bride revealed as ruling Spirit-baptized Christians in white raiment.
- The Bible symbolizes a thousand years as the period of Spirit baptized priests and kings ruling our earth since Jesus left.

An important key to understanding Revelation is learning that the earth spoken of in judgment is symbolized as Jerusalem, and it sits upon the seas (nations).

The earth is the Lord's, and the fulness thereof; the world, and they that dwell therein.

For he hath founded it upon the seas, and established it upon the floods.

Who shall ascend into the hill of the Lord? or who shall stand in his holy place?...
Lift up your heads, O ye gates; and be ye lift up, ye everlasting doors; and the King of glory shall come in.

— **Psalm 24:1-3,7**

This undoubtedly symbolizes Jerusalem and the temple as the earth. The "hill-holy place" refers to where the temple stood on Mt. Moriah. There are not any "gates" or "doors" that we know as part of our earth that the "King of Glory" (Jesus) came into except those in Jerusalem and the temple.

When we refer to these symbol descriptions, Revelation makes sense, as history records the judgment from God upon the earth (temple and Jerusalem).

John is the person to whom God gave access into the spiritual realm and who documents for us all the things he saw and experienced through spiritual visions—what will soon happen to the false Jewish people. He then contrasts it with the bride dressed in white raiment.

The Romans exiled John to the Isle of Patmos after the Jewish leaders, and Romans couldn't shut him up from teaching the NT resurrection of Jesus. Apparently, the Romans tried to execute him but were miraculously unsuccessful.

Most modern religionists have said John wrote the book around AD 95 because certain historians stated John was on Patmos during the Emperor Domitian's reign, AD 81–96. It could be possible John was still on Patmos then, but he more likely wrote Revelation *before* the Jewish Wars from AD 66–70.

These same religionists claim Domitian persecuted Christians and, therefore, John, because John says he was "in tribulation". However, the true church was in tribulation since Jesus left and still is today. Domitian had many from his army and administration executed but didn't single out specific Christians.

If John wrote Revelation before AD 66, he would have been in his late fifties or sixties. If during Domitian's reign, John would have been in his late eighties or nineties. It seems more probable he wrote it earlier. In addition, the angel tells John to measure the temple, which would not have existed after AD 70. Although, arguably, it could be the spiritual temple in heaven.

However, the leading argument for writing Revelation before AD 66 is the greatest catastrophic events in Jewish history first happened between AD 66-74 with the end of the temple worship system and the OT. It is more than likely he would have mentioned it at least once as historical accuracy or evidence if he wrote Revelation during Domitian's reign.

In fact, no one in the NT mentions a word about the destructive judgment as historical. Therefore, it also is more than likely all the NT writers wrote their scriptures before AD 66 as many mention or prophesy, the judgment is soon coming.

The Futurists have stated the book concerns our last days, and we can witness Revelation unfold in our lifetime. In addition, they followed false doctrines and passed along hearsay stating during these last days there would be a seven-year tribulation with an antichrist, a false prophet, and a revived Roman Empire through the European Union. We showed how the revived Empire is the Roman Catholic Church. They filtered their scriptural interpretations through false doctrines and twisted Scriptures to support their teachings.

So how did the false end-time doctrine get started? The Roman religion managed these end-time false doctrines after John Wycliffe and others translated the Latin Vulgate into English and more people could read and understand what was in the Scriptures.

Eventually, the Reformers (or Protest-tants) taught the "whore on the beast" in Revelation was the antichrist popes and the Roman church.

At first glance, this interpretation commits the false church to this description because of their mystic religious rites and idols incorporated into their church hierarchy. However, they are just a major part of the idol-worshiping belief system from Babylon.

To relieve the Roman church from the Reformers' attack of whoredom or antichrist, the false church convened the Council of Trent as a counterattack.

In order to keep the revived Roman Empire growing despite the negative Reformist teaching, the militant Society of Jesus, or Jesuit Priests, formed to enslave and convert people in many countries to Catholicism.

One of these priests, named Francisco Ribera, created a false doctrine that would push Daniel and Revelation's prophecies to the end of our time, taking the focus off the false church as the whore on the beast.

Ribera's doctrine then spread throughout Europe and, later, with other false doctrines into the seminaries around the world. Most church leaders today still teach these false doctrines, adopted from the false church.

Instead, what we will discover is that much of Revelation is different spiritual perspectives from OT history and in John's time, showing why the judgment was necessary.

In Leviticus 26, after Moses received the Ten Commandments, the LORD God told His people how He would bless them through His covenant(s). He then told them the judgments that would come if they remained unfaithful.

The latter of this Leviticus chapter, including portions of the books of Jeremiah and Ezekiel, often reads the same with the judgment events in Revelation. God wanted to bless His spiritual wife, and if she remained faithful to Him, He would. Instead, she repeatedly committed spiritual adultery by chasing after Babylonian inspired idols and their gods and goddesses.

> *Can a maid forget her ornaments, or a bride her attire? yet my people have forgotten me days without number.*
>
> – Jeremiah 2:32

> *And I saw, when for all the causes whereby backsliding Israel committed adultery I had put her away, and given her a bill of divorce; yet her treacherous sister Judah feared not, but went and played the harlot also.*
> *And it came to pass through the lightness of her whoredom, that she defiled the land, and committed adultery with stones and with stocks.*
>
> – Jeremiah 3:8-9

> *Surely as a wife treacherously departeth from her husband, so have ye dealt treacherously with me, O house of Israel, saith the Lord.*
>
> – Jeremiah 3:20

> *Turn, O backsliding children, saith the Lord; for I am married unto you: and I will take you one of a city, and two of a family, and I will bring you to Zion.*
>
> – Jeremiah 3:14

These verses help us understand the theme of Revelation, Israel's divorce, judgment, and destruction. The Romans and her allies leveled most of Jerusalem's walls and their temple. The Jews also destroyed themselves with Zealot infighting and starvation. After the destruction of the temple in AD 70 (the end of Daniel's prophecies), the Romans killed or enslaved those who survived or deported them to other countries.

Revelation

Before a pagan Jesuit priest created the false end-of-time doctrines, many scholars taught Revelation was more or less describing a spiritual contrast. It showed the harlot/woman OT Jews/Israel and the NT church or Jesus' spiritual bride, dressed in white raiment. Jesus released His kingdom and Spirit into baptized believers.

Most people have never learned how catastrophic these Revelation events were in heaven and earth. God shows us seven (sevens of) judgments of destruction brought upon the land (Israel) and earth (Jerusalem and temple) and islands (villages) and the sea (Roman Empire).

We see the reasons the Jews suffered destruction through the workings of seven churches. The plan and preparation (opening description of seven seals), then the announcement (seven trumpets), and finally, the execution poured out (seven vials or bowls of wrath). He also warns us of a false belief system within the world, Mystery Babylon, which the Jewish temple adopted, and how His Spirit instilled within us saves us (the bride) from the deceptive religions.

John says in the beginning verse of Revelation who is giving him the information and when the events will occur. Let's begin.

The Revelation of Jesus Christ, which God gave unto him, to shew unto his servants things which must shortly come to pass; and he sent and signified it by his angel unto his servant John.

- Revelation 1:1

This is clear John receives the Revelation message for *his* time, not our end time. It is apparent he spent years preaching to and building churches in a portion of Asia (now Turkey), as the message is for his servants.

John says an angel (messenger) revealed the revelation, "which must shortly come to pass". The Lord's angel, or messenger, will give John signs (or symbols) for what happened inside God's spiritual kingdom so he can understand what is about to happen, and then reveal it to his servants, the seven churches.

This prophecy is a blessing to whoever reads and understands it and again emphasizes the nearness of the prophecy, "for the time is at hand". A new blessing will come once the reader discovers the spiritual realism revealed from the OT.

Blessed is he that readeth, and they that hear the words of this prophecy, and keep those things which are written therein: for the time is at hand. John to the seven churches which are in Asia: Grace be unto you, and peace, from him which is, and which was, and which is to come; and from the seven Spirits which are before his throne.

- Revelation 1:3-4

The Revelation Happened

God used the number *seven* extensively throughout the Bible. It means completion or no more are needed for the situation.

Many people think God is an old-looking grandpa sitting on a literal throne and occasionally flicks his finger to shoot out a bolt of lightning.

Here, God displays His Spirit in seven spirits (v:4). No more are necessary to display His character of wisdom, understanding, counsel, might, knowledge, fear of the Lord, and righteousness (Isaiah 11:2-4).

In verse 9, John says he is a "companion in tribulation". All the true church was a companion in tribulation, defending their truth against the false Jews and the likes of Simon Magus and others. It is still in tribulation today, trying to teach the gospel of Jesus to an unbelieving and deceived world.

God can present Himself in any manner He chooses, hence the Father, Son, and Holy Spirit or in this case, the Alpha and Omega (vv: 11-16).

For the people still struggling with end-time false prophets who teach Revelation is about our time, all we need is common sense as we read further.

This shows the deception presented by false doctrines that teach Revelation concerns our last days and events of a seven-year tribulation, antichrist, and so on, because these events are about to happen in a few years for the seven churches to witness.

We can easily break out of their deception as we read Revelation.

1. We saw the events will "shortly come to pass", and the "time is at hand".

2. The message is to seven churches in Asia, not us, although religions today should learn from the warnings.

3. We will see John is in the Spirit or seeing things in the spirit realm, and how it relates to the end of the OT, the destruction of Jerusalem, and the temple.

Then we see how the harlot temple/Jerusalem contrasts with the bride. We will find out seven churches were allowing Satan inspired Gnostic-Babylonian idol worship, and sexual deviance (Jezebel spirit or perhaps Helen of Tyre) to enter their churches.

Through confronting these churches with warnings, God will show what the Jews did over centuries that are bringing an end to their city and temple. He then shows them the blessings to come if they repent and remain faithful.

John reveals something that religions have failed to teach us. If instead of building religious empires, imagine what could have been if they allowed Jesus to build His church.

All born again Spirit baptized persons are now kings and priests. What if they all woke up to this and realized they have gifts from God to change our world and lead people out of deception and darkness?

And from Jesus Christ, who is the faithful witness, and the first begotten of the dead, and the prince of the kings of the earth. Unto him that loved us, and washed us from our sins in his own blood, And hath made us kings and priests unto God and his Father; to him be glory and dominion for ever and ever. Amen.

– **Revelation 1:5,6**

For to one is given by the Spirit the word of wisdom; to another the word of knowledge by the same Spirit;
To another faith by the same Spirit; to another the gifts of healing by the same Spirit;
To another the working of miracles; to another prophecy; to another discerning of spirits; to another divers kinds of tongues; to another the interpretation of tongues:

- **1 Corinthians 12:8-10**

Our world could be so much different if churches would reveal these scriptures to us and assist everyone in exercising their gifts (wisdom, word of knowledge, faith, healing, miracles, prophecy, discerning spirits, different tongues and interpretation), instead of burdening us with their controlling religious domination of rites and rules.

John begins with a few signs to introduce us to Revelation's spiritual meanings, and we show the symbols are from the OT.

Behold, he cometh with clouds; and every eye shall see him, and they also which pierced him: and all kindreds of the earth shall wail because of him. Even so, Amen.

– Revelation 1:7

And I turned to see the voice that spake with me. And being turned, I saw seven golden candlesticks.

– Revelation 1:12

And he had in his right hand seven stars: and out of his mouth went a sharp two-edged sword: and his countenance was as the sun shineth in his strength.

– Revelation 1:16

The first signs are clouds, seven candlesticks, seven stars, and a sharp, two-edged sword. The Jews already knew from the OT that when the prophets declared judgment as clouds coming, it was a sign from God that the Jews or their enemies were in for trouble (Deuteronomy 4:11, 2 Samuel 22:12, Psalm 18:11-12).

All those who had a hand in the piercing (crucifixion) of Jesus would now experience and wail from His judgment and know it is Jesus carrying out their destruction in the earth, Jerusalem.

Since John wrote Revelation around thirty years after Jesus left, many who had Him crucified would see His judgment come upon them. As shown later, Josephus also records witnesses seeing Him, chariots, and angels in the clouds over Jerusalem when the judgment began.

Judgment is clouds...

Clouds and darkness are round about him: righteousness and judgment are the habitation of his throne.

- Psalm 97:2

Behold, he shall come up as clouds, and his chariots shall be as a whirlwind: his horses are swifter than eagles. Woe unto us! for we are spoiled.

- Jeremiah 4:13

John then explains the seven stars and the seven candlesticks. The two-edged sword is the Word of God, where one side reveals the truth or righteousness to our innermost being, and the other edge—judgment for not accepting the truth or that Jesus is God.

The seven stars are the angels of the seven churches: and the seven candlesticks which thou sawest are the seven churches.

- Revelation 1:20

For the word of God is quick, and powerful, and sharper than any two-edged sword, piercing even to the dividing asunder of soul and spirit, and of the joints and marrow, and is a discerner of the thoughts and intents of the heart.

- Hebrews 4:12

For each church, we will first see how His Word describes Him, the sword then divides what the seven churches are doing right and wrong, and the blessings if they repent (turn away from the mystic Babylonian rituals, relics, and worship).

Jesus will point out the good things each of the seven churches is doing, but will not tolerate them bringing in pagan activities.

The point made later in Revelation is the Jews did what these seven churches are doing, mixing Mystery Babylon in with their relationship with God, which caused their judgment (v19).

Churches today must heed these serious warnings if they bring Babylonian symbols (adornments) or their belief systems into their churches and our lives.

Don Nordstrom

Revelation 2

To the angel of the church in Ephesus.
The description of Jesus:

These things saith he that holdeth the seven stars in his right hand, who walketh in the midst of the seven golden candlesticks.

— Revelation 2:1

The good:

I know thy works, and thy labour, and thy patience, and how thou canst not bear them which are evil: and thou hast tried them which say they are apostles, and are not, and hast found them liars: And hast borne, and hast patience, and for my name's sake hast laboured, and hast not fainted.

— Revelation 2:2-3

The bad:

Nevertheless I have somewhat against thee, because thou hast left thy first love. Remember therefore from whence thou art fallen, and repent, and do the first works; or else I will come unto thee quickly, and will remove thy candlestick out of his place, except thou repent. But this thou hast, that thou hatest the deeds of the Nicolaitanes, which I also hate.

(The Nicolaitans were a sect of Gnostic's.)

- Revelation 2:4-6

The promised blessing if they repent:

He that hath an ear, let him hear what the Spirit saith unto the churches; To him that overcometh will I give to eat of the tree of life, which is in the midst of the paradise of God.

- Revelation 2:7

Church of Smyrna.
The description of Jesus:

These things saith the first and the last, which was dead, and is alive.

- Revelation 2:8

The good:

I know thy works, and tribulation, and poverty, (but thou art rich) and I know the blasphemy of them which say they are Jews, and are not, but are the synagogue of Satan.

(Therefore, judgment came upon the false Jews because they became the synagogue of Satan.)

- Revelation 2:9

The bad:

Fear none of those things which thou shalt suffer: behold, the devil shall cast some of you into prison, that ye may be tried; and ye shall have tribulation ten days.

– Revelation 2:10

The promised blessing:

Be thou faithful unto death, and I will give thee a crown of life. He that hath an ear, let him hear what the Spirit saith unto the churches; He that overcometh shall not be hurt of the second death.

– Revelation 2:10-11

Church of Pergamos.
The description of Jesus:

These things saith he which hath the sharp sword with two edges.

– Revelation 2:12

The good:

I know thy works, and where thou dwellest, even where Satan's seat is: and thou holdest fast my name, and hast not denied my faith, even in those days wherein Antipas was my faithful martyr, who was slain among you, where Satan dwelleth.

– Revelation 2:13

The bad:

But I have a few things against thee, because thou hast there them that hold the doctrine of Balaam, who taught Balac to cast a stumbling block before the children of Israel,

> *to eat things sacrificed unto idols, and to commit fornication. So hast thou also them that hold the doctrine of the Nicolaitanes, which thing I hate. Repent; or else I will come unto thee quickly, and will fight against them with the sword of my mouth.*
>
> *– Revelation 2:14–16*

The promised blessing:

> *He that hath an ear, let him hear what the Spirit saith unto the churches; To him that overcometh will I give to eat of the hidden manna,*
> *and will give him a white stone, and in the stone a new name written, which no man knoweth saving he that receiveth it.*
>
> *– Revelation 2:17*

Church of Thyatira.
The description of Jesus:

> *These things saith the Son of God, who hath his eyes like unto a flame of fire, and his feet are like fine brass.*
>
> *– Revelation 2:18*

The good:

> *I know thy works, and charity, and service, and faith, and thy patience, and thy works; and the last to be more than the first.*
>
> *– Revelation 2:19*

The bad:

> *Notwithstanding I have a few things against thee, because thou sufferest that woman Jezebel, which calleth herself a prophetess,*

> *to teach and to seduce my servants to commit fornication, and to eat things sacrificed unto idols.*
> *And I gave her space to repent of her fornication; and she repented not. Behold, I will cast her into a bed, and them that commit adultery with her into great tribulation, except they repent of their deeds.*
> *And I will kill her children with death; and all the churches shall know that I am he which searcheth the reins and hearts: and I will give unto every one of you according to your works.*

(Jezebel represents a woman (2 Kings 9:22) who seduces the Jews into worshiping [fornication] with idols, and perhaps here was Helen of Tyre.)

– Revelation 2:20–23

The promised blessing:

> *But unto you I say, and unto the rest in Thyatira, as many as have not this doctrine, and which have not known the depths of Satan, as they speak; I will put upon you none other burden. But that which ye have already hold fast till I come.*
> *And he that overcometh, and keepeth my works unto the end, to him will I give power over the nations: And he shall rule them with a rod of iron; as the vessels of a potter shall they be broken to shivers: even as I received of my Father.*
> *And I will give him the morning star. He that hath an ear, let him hear what the Spirit saith unto the churches.*

– Revelation 2:24–29

Don Nordstrom

Revelation 3

The church of Sardis.
The description of Jesus:

These things saith he that hath the seven Spirits of God, and the seven stars.

— ***Revelation 3:1***

The good:

I know thy works, that thou hast a name that thou livest, and art dead. Be watchful, and strengthen the things which remain, that are ready to die.

— ***Revelation 3:1-2***

The bad:

> *For I have not found thy works perfect before God. Remember therefore how thou hast received and heard, and hold fast, and repent.*
>
> *If therefore thou shalt not watch, I will come on thee as a thief, and thou shalt not know what hour I will come upon thee.*

- Revelation 3:2-3

The promised blessing:

> *Thou hast a few names even in Sardis which have not defiled their garments; and they shall walk with me in white: for they are worthy. He that overcometh, the same shall be clothed in white raiment; and I will not blot out his name out of the book of life, but I will confess his name before my Father, and before his angels. He that hath an ear, let him hear what the Spirit saith unto the churches.*

- Revelation 3:4-6

The church of Philadelphia.
The description of Jesus:

> *These things saith he that is holy, he that is true, he that hath the key of David, he that openeth, and no man shutteth; and shutteth, and no man openeth.*

- Revelation 3:7

The good:

> *I know thy works: behold, I have set before thee an open door, and no man can shut it: for thou hast a little strength, and hast kept my word, and hast not denied my name.*

Behold, I will make them of the synagogue of Satan, which say they are Jews, and are not, but do lie; behold, I will make them to come and worship before thy feet, and to know that I have loved thee.

Because thou hast kept the word of my patience, I also will keep thee from the hour of temptation, which shall come upon all the world, to try them that dwell upon the earth.

Behold, I come quickly: hold that fast which thou hast, that no man take thy crown.

— **Revelation 3:8-11**

The bad:
Nothing.
The promised blessing:

Him that overcometh will I make a pillar in the temple of my God, and he shall go no more out: and I will write upon him the name of my God, and the name of the city of my God, which is new Jerusalem, which cometh down out of heaven from my God: and I will write upon him my new name. He that hath an ear, let him hear what the Spirit saith unto the churches.

— **Revelation 3:12-13**

The church of Laodicea.
The description of Jesus:

These things saith the Amen, the faithful and true witness, the beginning of the creation of God.

— **Revelation 3:14**

The good:
Nothing.

The bad:

> *I know thy works, that thou art neither cold nor hot: I would thou wert cold or hot.*
>
> *So then because thou art lukewarm, and neither cold nor hot, I will spue thee out of my mouth.*
>
> *Because thou sayest, I am rich, and increased with goods, and have need of nothing; and knowest not that thou art wretched, and miserable, and poor, and blind, and naked:*

— Revelation 3:15-17

The promised blessing:

> *I counsel thee to buy of me gold tried in the fire, that thou mayest be rich; and white raiment, that thou mayest be clothed,*
>
> *and that the shame of thy nakedness do not appear; and anoint thine eyes with eyesalve, that thou mayest see.*
>
> *As many as I love, I rebuke and chasten: be zealous therefore, and repent. Behold, I stand at the door, and knock: if any man hear my voice, and open the door, I will come in to him, and will sup with him, and he with me.*
>
> *To him that overcometh will I grant to sit with me in my throne, even as I also overcame, and am set down with my Father in his throne. He that hath an ear, let him hear what the Spirit saith unto the churches.*

— Revelation 3:18-22

What we read were the messages to seven churches in Asia concerning their actions, or lack thereof. Jesus lets them know they are mixing pagan teachings into their churches.

The Revelation Happened

This stems from Gnostic Mystery Babylon. We learn it is from the synagogue of Satan.

The rest of Revelation can confuse even the brightest scholar if we do not understand the symbolism is from the OT. It is spiritual symbolism, which most futurists have trouble discerning.

We will see periods of 1,260 days, 42 months, and as "time, times, and half a time." The latter period is a symbol for an appointed time, then more than one (times), but then dividing the time (See *Strong's Concordance*, Hebrew #5732 and #6387).

After Jesus's resurrection, there were three major Jewish wars against the Romans. Each of these revolts lasted approximately 1,260 days, 42 months, or three and one-half years, and it's probable the above periods show and divide each revolt into three and one-half years.

During the first Jewish revolt, there was a civil war within Jerusalem. The Romans dealt with their own temporary civil war, determining who would take Nero's place after his supposed death. (Some historians believe he faked his suicide to avoid execution and became a traveling actor and musician)

The judgment on Jerusalem not only came externally, but also internally.

There were many countries and participants in these wars, and trying to figure out who the symbolized players are is difficult. The internal Zealots were often as cruel as the Romans (west), and they also played a part in the symbolism along with the Syrians from the north, Arabians from the east, and Idumeans from the south. (Four Winds)

The first war took place in approximately AD 66–70. Jerusalem suffered destruction, and the Romans burned and brought the temple buildings to the ground.

The second revolt followed in approximately late AD 70–74, when a sect of Zealots, the Sicarii, escaped to a plateau named Masada, where Herod's palace had stood. (They later committed suicide by their swords so as not to be slaughtered by the Romans).

The third revolt happened in approximately AD 132–135, during the Roman Emperor Hadrian's reign. Hadrian and a remnant of Jews had somewhat restored Jerusalem. Hadrian destroyed the remaining Jerusalem, and the Jews scattered.

An additional uprising took place in AD 115 from Jewish slaves in Egypt, (along with other Jewish insurrections in Greece, Cyprus, and Libya), but it's not believed to be part of this prophecy because the revolts did not happen in Israel.

(**Note:** With the chance of confusing readers, we can achieve a deeper understanding of Revelation by viewing it knowing that the spirit realm first underwent a destruction, judgment, and restoration. Lucifer with his followers had almost brought God's kingdom into complete darkness (Genesis 1:2).

In God's world, there is a heaven, an earth, and a sea where the enemies of God went before flushing into the creation of our universe. It is then obvious that this requires a different teaching structure presented to us than from religious teachers. It would show, for example, Genesis 1 and chapter is not the creation of our heaven and earth, but the formation, destruction, and restoration (New Heaven and New Earth) of God's world.

It is not the intent to bring this alternative study into this book, and certainly we could reject this interpretation and still achieve a complete understanding of the history involved in Revelation. However, Revelation is easier to understand knowing John sees the *spiritual* heaven, earth, sea, temple and so on.

In addition, this book just shows the key participants and events in the Revelation judgments. But seeing the spiritual judgment first and then the resulting physical judgment from it, the reader receives a deeper understanding of Revelation).

Revelation 4

After this I looked, and, behold, a door was opened in heaven: and the first voice which I heard was as it were of a trumpet talking with me; which said, Come up hither, and I will shew thee things which must be hereafter. And immediately I was in the spirit: and, behold, a throne was set in heaven, and one sat on the throne.

And he that sat was to look upon like a jasper and a sardine stone: and there was a rainbow round about the throne, in sight like unto an emerald.

And round about the throne were four and twenty seats: upon the seats I saw four and twenty elders sitting, clothed in white raiment; and they had on their heads crowns of gold.

And out of the throne proceeded lightnings and thunderings and voices: and there were seven lamps of fire burning before the throne, which are the seven Spirits of God.

— **Revelation 4:1-5**

We saw what was happening in the seven churches, now we will see what comes hereafter with the judgments.

John is in the spirit realm, and sees a door open in heaven, which reveals the throne room. It is the same general description Ezekiel (ch. 1) saw when God revealed His throne room to him (except the 24 elders were not resurrected yet) including the spiritual rainbow from the flood.

John sees and hears:

- The spiritual realm and hears a voice as a trumpet (announcement).
- The throne room, and the beings that exist therein, with the sounds and activities. The seven spirits of fire describe God from Isaiah 11.
- The throne is a judge's seat, with the cherubim and seraphim giving honor, just as we call a judge "Your Honor".
- Twenty-four crowned elders, ruling as kings and priests (Revelation 1:6). These redeemed (white raiment) elders are from the OT as witnesses, wearing crowns as rewards for their faithfulness.

Gather unto me all the elders of your tribes, and your officers, that I may speak these words in their ears, and call heaven and earth to record against them.

— **Deuteronomy 31:28**

Verse 11 says all things were created for His pleasure. There is no more disappointment or heartache in heaven. All we will know is joy and pleasure in all we do and experience.

Revelation 5

In Revelation 5, we see a book with seven seals. The spiritual picture of Jesus describes Him as the *Lion of Judah* and the *Root of David*.

John can see all the events here because there is no time in eternity, which is why he sees the spiritual images of Jesus as a sacrificial lamb along with, or as, the conquering Lion of Judah and Root of David.

> *And one of the elders saith unto me, Weep not: behold, the Lion of the tribe of Judah, the Root of David, hath prevailed to open the book, and to loose the seven seals thereof.*
> *And I beheld, and, lo, in the midst of the throne and of the four beasts, and in the midst of the elders, stood a Lamb as it had been slain, having seven horns and seven eyes, which are the seven Spirits of God sent forth into all the earth.*
>
> **– Revelation 5:5–6**

We remember God is Spirit, and can present Himself in any form He chooses. There is nothing hidden in God. When we shall gaze upon Him, we will see the depth of His character and nature, constantly revolving or cycling before our eyes.

A hand reveals a book (scroll). This is the same book from Ezekiel's prophecy when God tells Ezekiel to prophesy against Israel.

And when I looked, behold, an hand was sent unto me; and, lo, a roll of a book was therein; And he spread it before me; and it was written within and without: and there was written therein lamentations, and mourning, and woe.

- Ezekiel 2:9-10

In addition, Leviticus 26 portrays the promises of God if His people will follow His commandments. If not, sevens of judgments will come upon them when Israel turns against God. This is what the seven seals and the contents represent, in both heaven and earth.

Again, we are told that we are kings and priests while on our earth. We do not need to die first, but are baptized now in the fire of the Holy Spirit to rule with the Kingdom of God.

John sees innumerable angels and the elders (v. 11), and all proclaim Jesus as the only one worthy to receive all power (to execute judgment) and blessings (receive His redeemed people).

We discover there is a spiritual earth and a sea in heaven (v. 13), and everyone sings a new song (presenting the NT).

The sea is temporary, and as we will later see, it no longer exists in heaven.

He will not execute the judgments until all the seals open, revealing the contents in the book as a scroll.

Revelation 6

And I saw when the Lamb opened one of the seals, and I heard, as it were the noise of thunder, one of the four beasts saying, Come and see.

- Revelation 6:1

Nothing happens without God allowing the event, whether blessing or destruction. The opening of the seals is setting the spirits in position to execute the judgments.

Four seals reveal four colored horses. Zechariah (1:8-11, and 6:2-8) learned the horses and chariots were four spirits from heaven that moved around the earth.

These horses (spirits) will go forth to allow the judgment from the Lord, which we will also see were warnings from the book of Leviticus.

The Roman Empire, the Zealots, and the surrounding countries are the destroyers.

The white horse is a conquering spirit.

> *And I saw, and behold a white horse: and he that sat on him had a bow; and a crown was given unto him: and he went forth conquering, and to conquer.*

> – *Revelation 6:2*

Relating Leviticus verses follow these passages.

> *And I will set my face against you, and ye shall be slain before your enemies: they that hate you shall reign over you; and ye shall flee when none pursueth you.*

> – *Leviticus 26:17*

> *And I will make your cities waste, and bring your sanctuaries unto desolation, and I will not smell the savour of your sweet odours.*

> – *Leviticus 26:31*

The next seal, a red horse, allows the Jews to kill each other, and there will be no peace. Jerusalem divided into three factions controlled by the Zealots—John, Eleazar, and Simon (not the apostles), and were a *pestilence* that rose against their own people. The Sicarri would come into Jerusalem with swords hidden under their clothing.

> *And there went out another horse that was red: and power was given to him that sat thereon to take peace from the earth, and that they should kill one another: and there was given unto him a great sword.*

> – *Revelation 6:4*

And I will bring a sword upon you, that shall avenge the quarrel of my covenant: and when ye are gathered together within your cities, I will send the pestilence among you; and ye shall be delivered into the hand of the enemy,

– **Leviticus 26:25**

When the third seal opens, the black horse will bring famine to the earth. Despite Israel having plenty of food, they could not get access to it, and the Zealots stole what food there was. Some victims turned to cannibalism, while thousands starved to death.

And when he had opened the third seal, I heard the third beast say, Come and see. And I beheld, and lo a black horse; and he that sat on him had a pair of balances in his hand. And I heard a voice in the midst of the four beasts say, A measure of wheat for a penny, and three measures of barley for a penny; and see thou hurt not the oil and the wine.

– **Revelation 6:5-6**

And your strength shall be spent in vain: for your land shall not yield her increase, neither shall the trees of the land yield their fruits.

– **Leviticus 26:20**

And when I have broken the staff of your bread, ten women shall bake your bread in one oven, and they shall deliver you your bread again by weight: and ye shall eat, and not be satisfied.

– **Leviticus 26:26**

And ye shall eat the flesh of your sons, and the flesh of your daughters shall ye eat.

– **Leviticus 26:29**

The fourth seal reveals a pale horse that allows death and hell, or eternal separation from God. Since "earth" represents Jerusalem and the temple, this describes how the Zealots (beasts of the earth) played their part in the destruction of Jerusalem.

And I looked, and behold a pale horse: and his name that sat on him was Death, and Hell followed with him. And power was given unto them over the fourth part of the earth, to kill with sword, and with hunger, and with death, and with the beasts of the earth.

– **Revelation 6:8**

I will also send wild beasts among you, which shall rob you of your children, and destroy your cattle, and make you few in number; and your high ways shall be desolate.

– **Leviticus 26:22**

And I will destroy your high places, and cut down your images, and cast your carcases upon the carcases of your idols, and my soul shall abhor you.

– **Leviticus 26:30**

And I will scatter you among the heathen, and will draw out a sword after you: and your land shall be desolate, and your cities waste.

– **Leviticus 26:33**

The fifth seal reveals those under the altar who for approximately the previous thirty years before John wrote Revelation had taught and revealed Jesus as the promised Messiah or Savior. The persecutors (temple leaders) had them killed for teaching the gospel (truth about Jesus).

During this time, the persecuted true church (white robes) included those stoned to death, their heads bashed in, or brought before the Romans by their own people for torture and crucifixion. They are now praying to the Lord to avenge their persecutions.

And they cried with a loud voice, saying, How long, O Lord, holy and true, dost thou not judge and avenge our blood on them that dwell on the earth?

– Revelation 6:10

In our courts today, the judge often will do nothing until the lawyers move (file motions) or ask the judge to decide. The early true church prayed for God to come with judgment on those who persecuted them to death. Those prayers are what moved God to execute His judgments (v 10).

Many people wonder why Jesus is tarrying today. It is because our tribulation has not yet moved us (we are not suffering enough) to pray for Jesus to come and deliver us. We need to do as the early true church did and pray for God to execute His judgments on this world.

The rest of this chapter shows the judgment-summary-language that comes from the OT. The temple (heaven on earth) and synagogues stored the scrolls of the OT, and are now symbolized as rolled up, moved, no longer needed (v 14).

It is probable a group of scribes in a synagogue preserved their scrolls in a cave until discovered in our time as the *Dead Sea Scrolls*.

The prophet Joel, in his 2nd book, first shows the destruction in Revelation, then the restoration of Israel (Joel 2:18–29), which occurred in our time (1948), before the last judgment. And God will save anyone in Israel who calls upon His name (v. 32).

The first judgment prophecy from Joel:

> *Blow ye the trumpet in Zion, and sound an alarm in my holy mountain: let all the inhabitants of the land tremble: for the day of the Lord cometh, for it is nigh at hand;*
> *A day of darkness and of gloominess, a day of clouds and of thick darkness, as the morning spread upon the mountains:*
> *a great people and a strong; there hath not been ever the like; neither shall be any more after it, even to the years of many generations.*

– Joel 2:1–2

The restoration in our time:

> *And I will restore to you the years that the locust hath eaten, the cankerworm, and the caterpiller, and the palmerworm, my great army which I sent among you.*
> *And ye shall eat in plenty, and be satisfied, and praise the name of the LORD your God, that hath dealt wondrously with you: and my people shall never be ashamed.*
> *And ye shall know that I am in the midst of Israel, and that I am the LORD your God, and none else: and my people shall never be ashamed.*

– Joel 2:25-27

The final judgment:

> *And I will shew wonders in the heavens and in the earth, blood, and fire, and pillars of smoke. The sun shall be turned into darkness, and the moon into blood, before the great and terrible day of the Lord come.*
>
> – Joel 2:30-31

In Flavius Josephus's historic book, *The Wars of the Jews*, he witnessed the verdict carried out against the false Jews.

Joel aptly prophesied what Josephus observed, the destruction of Jerusalem and Israel as it went up in flames.

The Zealot John (not the apostle) would enter towns and rile the people to go to war. Once the Romans conquered these towns, John's sect of Zealots would escape to another town, lying as a false prophet of false conquests. He would deceive others to fight. Those who wouldn't, his Zealots would rob them of their last bits of food, often killing them if caught hiding it.

Roman legions had taken their own casualties, so their generals tactfully offered peace before marching into towns.

Inhabitants in Jerusalem, thinking their three walls (deep) and their temple well-fortified, while listening to John (Zealot) telling them God was on their side, would go to war until the Romans had them surrender or killed. The Romans would take some conquered Jews as slaves to fight alongside with the soldiers against their fellow Jewish people.

The surviving temple kings and Zealot leaders hid in the mountains and dens until the Romans discovered and captured them.

Don Nordstrom

Revelation 7

What John sees next are four angels holding back the four winds (surrounding countries), prepared to execute their destruction from all directions on the earth (Jerusalem) and the sea (the Roman Empire). The trees are the Jewish servants of God who became Christians (Isaiah 61:3).

The Roman armies and allies had Jerusalem surrounded for many months, but did not attack from the east until the Roman general and later emperor Titus attacked the eastern gate and wall.

An angel from the east commands that the judgments cannot begin until they seal the foreheads (with the Holy Spirit) of God's servants. This would remind the readers of one of Ezekiel's prophecies.

> *And the Lord said unto him, Go through the midst of the city, through the midst of Jerusalem, and set a mark upon the foreheads of the men that sigh and that cry for all the abominations that be done in the midst thereof.*

And to the others he said in mine hearing, Go ye after him through the city, and smite: let not your eye spare, neither have ye pity:
Slay utterly old and young, both maids, and little children, and women: but come not near any man upon whom is the mark; and begin at my sanctuary. Then they began at the ancient men which were before the house.

– **Ezekiel 9:4-6**

Although their destruction eventually occurs, God first saves those Jewish people symbolically represented from all tribes. Every Jewish person had the opportunity to receive the mark or seal of the Holy Spirit.

For I am not ashamed of the gospel of Christ: for it is the power of God unto salvation to every one that believeth; to the Jew first, and also to the Greek.

– **Romans 1:16**

In verse 4, the sealed number represents twelve thousand each of the twelve tribes of Israel (144,000). It will symbolize all the Jewish tribes in heaven.

John then sees all Spirit-baptized Christians (v 9), Jewish and non-Jewish, out of our historical great tribulation; wearing white robes, washed with the blood of the Lamb. They remained faithful during their tribulation lives, and now Jesus will care for them forever. There will be no more sorrow in His kingdom.

(Again, we recommend reading Josephus's historic book, The Wars of the Jews (WOJ), particular, Books III and onward. Find it free online at Project Gutenberg.[3] We will provide excerpts concerning the judgments from his book as they relate to Revelation).

Revelation 8

And when he had opened the seventh seal, there was silence in heaven about the space of half an hour.

– **Revelation 8:1**

> "And at the ninth hour of the night, so great a light shone round the altar and the holy house, that it appeared to be bright day time; which lasted for half an hour. This light seemed to be a good sign to the unskillful, but was so interpreted by the sacred scribes, as to portend those events that followed immediately upon it."
> (WOJ Book 6, Chapter 5.3)

John notices silence in heaven. God gives the Jews one last chance to repent before the judgments begin.

And I saw the seven angels which stood before God; and to them were given seven trumpets.

And another angel came and stood at the altar, having a golden censer; and there was given unto him much incense, that he should offer it with the prayers of all saints upon the golden altar which was before the throne.

And the smoke of the incense, which came with the prayers of the saints, ascended up before God out of the angel's hand. And the angel took the censer, and filled it with fire of the altar, and cast it into the earth: and there were voices, and thunderings, and lightnings, and an earthquake.

- ***Revelation 8:1-4***

Satan mocked God and created his own kingdom throne rooms in our world, within pagan temples. Just as our prayers are like incense, worshipers of Caesar and other gods offered up incense, which demonstrated their allegiance to Satan.

"That they lay all night before the wall, though in a very bad encampment; for there broke out a prodigious storm in the night, with the utmost violence, and very strong winds, with the largest showers of rain, with continued lightnings, terrible thunderings, and amazing concussions and bellowings of the earth, that was in an earthquake. These things were a manifest indication that some destruction was coming upon men, when the system of the world was put into this disorder; and any one would guess that these wonders foreshowed some grand calamities that were coming."

(WOJ Book 4, Chapter 4.5)

"The events that followed it of so considerable a nature as to deserve such signals; for, before sun-setting, chariots and troops of soldiers in their armor were seen running about among the clouds, and surrounding of cities. Moreover, at that feast which we call Pentecost,

> *as the priests were going by night into the inner [court of the temple,] as their custom was, to perform their sacred ministrations, they said that, in the first place, they felt a quaking, and heard a great noise, and after that they heard a sound as of a great multitude, saying, "Let us remove hence.""*
>
> (WOJ Book 6, Chapter 5.3)

We can look back at Ezekiel's prophecy again since he foresees the plagues, and in this case, in thirds.

> *Thou shalt burn with fire a third part in the midst of the city, when the days of the siege are fulfilled: and thou shalt take a third part, and smite about it with a knife:*
> *and a third part thou shalt scatter in the wind; and I will draw out a sword after them.*
>
> **– Ezekiel 5:2**

And again, in Revelation...

> *The first angel sounded, and there followed hail and fire mingled with blood, and they were cast upon the earth:*
> *and the third part of trees was burnt up, and all green grass was burnt up.*
>
> **– Revelation 8:7**

The Romans had catapults that "hailed" stones of fire onto Jerusalem.

> *"Vespasian [first a general then emperor of Rome] then set the engines [catapults and crossbows] for throwing stones and darts round about the city. The number of the engines was in all a hundred and sixty... such engines as were intended for that purpose threw at once*

lances upon them with a great noise, and stones [as hail] of the weight of a talent [about 80lbs] were thrown by the engines that were prepared for that purpose, together with fire, and a vast multitude of arrows, which made the wall so dangerous, that the Jews durst not only not come upon it, but durst not come to those parts within the walls which were reached by the engines; for the multitude of the Arabian archers, as well also as all those that threw darts and slung stones, fell to work at the same time with the engines."

[words in brackets added by author]
(WOJ Book 3, Chapter 7.9)

"So [Vespasian] repelled the Jews in great measure by the Arabian archers, and the Syrian slingers, and by those that threw stones at them, nor was there any intermission of the great number of their offensive engines."
(WOJ Book 3, Chapter 7.18)

And the second angel sounded, and as it were a great mountain burning with fire was cast into the sea: and the third part of the sea became blood;
And the third part of the creatures which were in the sea, and had life, died; and the third part of the ships were destroyed.

- Revelation 8:8-9

The mountain is a symbol of authority and probably represents the temple mount under destruction (Matthew 21:21). The temple was under judgment (fire) from God.

We shall see in Revelation 10 the sea symbolically refers to the Roman Empire, which also surrounded the literal Mediterranean Sea.

Although the sevens of judgments in Revelation mainly concern the destruction of Jerusalem and the temple, the devastation also included the surrounding area or empire, including the creatures and bloodshed throughout the empire. Many also tried to escape by the literal seas.

> "And there dashed their ships one against another, and dashed some of them against the rocks, and carried many of them by force, while they strove against the opposite waves, into the main sea; for the shore was so rocky, and had so many of the enemy upon it, that they were afraid to come to land; nay, the waves rose so very high, that they drowned them; nor was there any place whither they could fly, nor any way to save themselves; while they were thrust out of the sea, by the violence of the wind, if they staid where they were, and out of the city by the violence of the Romans. And much lamentation there was when the ships were dashed against one another, and a terrible noise when they were broken to pieces; and some of the multitude that were in them were covered with waves, and so perished, and many were embarrassed with shipwrecks. But some of them thought that to die by their own swords was lighter than by the sea, and so they killed themselves before they were drowned; although the greatest part of them were carried by the waves, and dashed to pieces against the abrupt parts of the rocks, insomuch that the sea was bloody a long way, and the maritime parts were full of dead bodies; for the Romans came upon those that were carried to the shore, and destroyed them; and the number of the bodies that were thus thrown out of the sea was four thousand and two hundred."
> (WOJ Book 3, Chapter 9.3)

And the third angel sounded, and there fell a great star from heaven, burning as it were a lamp, and it fell upon the third part of the rivers, and upon the fountains of waters;
And the name of the star is called Wormwood: and the third part

> *of the waters became wormwood; and many men died of the waters, because they were made bitter.*

> **– Revelation 8:10-11**

The Zealots and other rebels attacked their own people and villages. Wormwood was a symbol of bitterness in the Jews, and waters are people (Revelation 17:15). It is saying a third part of Jewish people became bitter and was a cause of their death. God made this description from the OT.

> *But her end is bitter as wormwood, sharp as a two-edged sword.*

> **– Proverbs 5:4**

> *Oh that my head were waters, and mine eyes a fountain of tears, that I might weep day and night for the slain of the daughter of my people!*

> **– Jeremiah 9:1**

> *Therefore thus saith the Lord of hosts, the God of Israel; Behold, I will feed them, even this people, with wormwood, and give them water of gall to drink.*

> **– Jeremiah 9:15**

"There were besides disorders and civil wars in every city; and all those that were at quiet from the Romans turned their hands one against another. There was also a **bitter** contest between those that were fond of war, and those that were desirous for peace. At the first this quarrelsome temper caught hold of private families, who could not agree among themselves; after which those people that were the dearest to one another brake through all restraints with regard to each other, and every one associated with those of his own opinion, and began already to stand in opposition one to another; so that seditions arose every where, while those that were for innovations, and were desirous of war, by their youth and boldness, were too hard for the aged and prudent men."

(WOJ Book 4, Chapter 3.2)

Verse 12 of this Revelation chapter once again shows the language of judgment warning, all too familiar to the OT Jews. It describes the beginning of the burning of the city. The smoke could blot out a third of the moon, stars, and the sun.

Verse 13 resembles what Josephus tells of a man who gave the final warning as the judgments took place. Angels are messengers, and the following messenger, named Jesus, gave plenty of warning and exemplified Jesus Christ in his life...

"But, what is still more terrible, there was one Jesus, the son of Ananus, a plebeian and a husbandman, who, four years before the war began, and at a time when the city was in very great peace and prosperity, came to that feast whereon it is our custom for every one to make tabernacles to God in the temple, began on a sudden to cry aloud,

"A voice from the east, a voice from the west, a voice from the four winds, a voice against Jerusalem and the holy house, a voice against the bridegrooms and the brides, and a voice against this whole people!"

This was his cry, as he went about by day and by night, in all the lanes of the city. However, certain of the most eminent among the populace had great indignation at this dire cry of his, and took up the man, and gave him a great number of severe stripes; yet did not he either say any thing for himself, or any thing peculiar to those that chastised him, but still went on with the same words which he cried before.

Hereupon our rulers, supposing, as the case proved to be, that this was a sort of divine fury in the man, brought him to the Roman procurator, where he was whipped till his bones were laid bare; yet he did not make any supplication for himself, nor shed any tears, but turning his voice to the most lamentable tone possible, at every stroke of the whip his answer was, "Woe, woe to Jerusalem!"

... Now, during all the time that passed before the war began, this man did not go near any of the citizens, nor was seen by them while he said so; but he every day uttered these lamentable words, as if it were his premeditated vow, "Woe, woe to Jerusalem!"

Nor did he give ill words to any of those that beat him every day, nor good words to those that gave him food; but this was his reply to all men, and indeed no other than a melancholy presage of what was to come.

This cry of his was the loudest at the festivals; and he continued this ditty for seven years and five months, without growing hoarse, or being tired therewith, until the very time that he saw his presage in earnest fulfilled in our siege, when it ceased; for as he was going round upon the wall, he cried out with his utmost force, "Woe, woe to the city again, and to the people, and to the holy house!" And just as he added at the last, "Woe, woe to myself also!" there came a stone out of one of the engines, and smote him, and killed him immediately; and as he was uttering the very same presages he gave up the ghost."

(WOJ Book 6, Chapter 5.3)

Revelation 9

An angel receives the key to the bottomless pit (hell or abyss) to release the demons unto Jerusalem. The armies that came out of the smoke were like a plague of locusts that surrounded Jerusalem—dressed for battle, preparing their armaments of destruction, shouting, and tormenting the Jews.

It is possible Revelation 9 begins with prophesying the fall of Nero, after Rome almost burned to the ground. Out of this burning destruction came the Roman legions like locusts to destroy Jerusalem and other cities.

We already know the Romans adopted the original Babylonian gods and goddesses, (just changed their names). It seems obvious then the Romans carried the Zodiac signs of the constellations, woman's hair (Virgo) lion's teeth (Leo) scorpions (Scorpio) and so forth. It shows the spiritual demons behind the attacking forces.

And the fifth angel sounded, and I saw a star fall from heaven unto the earth: and to him was given the key of the bottomless pit.

And he opened the bottomless pit; and there arose a smoke out of the pit, as the smoke of a great furnace; and the sun and the air were darkened by reason of the smoke of the pit. And there came out of the smoke locusts upon the earth: and unto them was given power, as the scorpions of the earth have power.

And it was commanded them that they should not hurt the grass of the earth, neither any green thing, neither any tree; but only those men which have not the seal of God in their foreheads.

And to them it was given that they should not kill them, but that they should be tormented five months: and their torment was as the torment of a scorpion, when he striketh a man. And in those days shall men seek death, and shall not find it; and shall desire to die, and death shall flee from them.

And the shapes of the locusts were like unto horses prepared unto battle; and on their heads were as it were crowns like gold, and their faces were as the faces of men.

And they had hair as the hair of women, and their teeth were as the teeth of lions. And they had breastplates, as it were breastplates of iron; and the sound of their wings was as the sound of chariots of many horses running to battle.

And they had tails like unto scorpions, and there were stings in their tails: and their power was to hurt men five months. And they had a king over them, which is the angel of the bottomless pit, whose name in the Hebrew tongue is Abaddon, but in the Greek tongue hath his name Apollyon.

– Revelation 9:1–11

We see the visual description of these spiritual demons as the destroyers gathered for battle.

While the Zealots were causing civil strife within the towns, the Romans would gather around and set up their camps.

For five months, the people could not leave without encountering the soldiers. Many people in Jerusalem starved to death, or the Zealots tortured them for not taking up arms against the soldiers. It would seem many people preferred death instead of the relentless suffering.

The Roman Legions marched with horses, and men hauled the "engines" on carriers, which were catapults with "sting in their tails".

They arrayed their horses with different armaments and the soldiers with several tools for fighting. All of this was to intimidate the Jews into surrender. Other countries also joined in and surrounded the cities.

> "The footmen are armed with breastplates and head-pieces, and have swords on each side; but the sword which is upon their left side is much longer than the other… Those foot-men also that are chosen out from the rest to be about the general himself have a lance and a buckler, but the rest of the foot soldiers have a spear and a long buckler, besides a saw and a basket, a pick-axe and an axe, a thong of leather and a hook
>
> … The horsemen have a long sword on their right sides, axed a long pole in their hand; a shield also lies by them obliquely on one side of their horses, with three or more darts that are borne in their quiver, having broad points, and not smaller than spears. They have also head-pieces and breastplates, in like manner as have all the footmen."
>
> (WOJ Book 3, Chapter 5.5)

The Romans had several "engines" as artillery at their disposal. From the spoils of war with the Greeks, they adapted their technology into formidable objects of destruction. They made some of these from different metals and included *ballistas*, *scorpios* (SCORPIONS), and battering rams, among others. They also used towers and ladders.

The ballista was like a large crossbow that could launch just about anything but typically shot large stones the size of a talent (about 80 lbs).

Another type used a crossbar that a tensioned spoke kicked with tremendous force. Then a catapult could shoot huge objects or stones, some of which they set on fire and would rain as a hail of fire upon the city.

Scorpions were a smaller crossbow-like weapon, from which arrows or smaller darts could pierce protective covering, then "sting" (stab) the occupant, causing great suffering. Soldiers often mounted these on towers, and darts from the scorpions were quite accurate.

Battering rams, identified as an iron face that appeared as a ram, could soon break down any wall. Soldiers first rammed the wall as a greeting, tormenting the people inside.

According to Roman law, people could surrender thereafter to this announcement, escaping death. Perhaps many Christians escaped at these times.

Abaddon, or Apollyon, describes a destroyer or destruction that only Satan and his followers could devise the means of torture and execution provided by the Zealots and the Romans.

> "The severity of the famine made [the Jews] bold in thus going out; so nothing remained but that, when they were concealed from the robbers, they should be taken by the enemy; …so they were first whipped, and then tormented with all sorts of tortures, before they died, and were then crucified before the wall of the city… while they caught every day five hundred Jews; nay, some days they caught more…

> So the soldiers, out of the wrath and hatred they bore the Jews, nailed those they caught, one after one way, and another after another, to the crosses, by way of jest, when their multitude was so great, that room was wanting for the crosses, and crosses wanting for the bodies."
> (WOJ Book 5, Chapter 11.1)

We had just seen the demonic forces from the abyss of Rome. Next, we see four angels bound in the river Euphrates released. They reveal the demonic forces behind the idols the Jews worshiped over the centuries.

> *And the sixth angel sounded, and I heard a voice from the four horns of the golden altar which is before God, Saying to the sixth angel which had the trumpet, Loose the four angels which are bound in the great river Euphrates.*
>
> *And the four angels were loosed, which were prepared for an hour, and a day, and a month, and a year, for to slay the third part of men. And the number of the army of the horsemen were two hundred thousand thousand: and I heard the number of them.*
>
> *And thus I saw the horses in the vision, and them that sat on them, having breastplates of fire, and of jacinth, and brimstone: and the heads of the horses were as the heads of lions; and out of their mouths issued fire and smoke and brimstone.*
>
> *By these three was the third part of men killed, by the fire, and by the smoke, and by the brimstone, which issued out of their mouths. For their power is in their mouth, and in their tails: for their tails were like unto serpents, and had heads, and with them they do hurt.*

And the rest of the men which were not killed by these plagues yet repented not of the works of their hands, that they should not worship devils, and idols of gold, and silver, and brass, and stone, and of wood: which neither can see, nor hear, nor walk:
Neither repented they of their murders, nor of their sorceries, nor of their fornication, nor of their thefts.

― ***Revelation 9:13-21***

Again, this is not literal, but another spiritual vision looking back in history, not forward. We already know the horses are spirits. The number here is not literal either, but symbolized as infinite demonic spirits, and not future Chinese armies, as some Futurists want us to believe.

It represents the demonic forces in the vision that controlled the Babylonian area since Nimrod first moved against God. We can know this because the horses (spirits) heads carry the emblem of a lion (Jeremiah 50:17).

From this unique perspective of judgment, verses 20 and 21, these Babylonian demons caused the judgment (fire) and torment (brimstone) upon the Jews. They are as plagues, and shows who the Jews worshiped as devils, through idols, and the curse of their doing without repenting over the centuries, brought this judgment.

Revelation 10

And I saw another mighty angel come down from heaven, clothed with a cloud: and a rainbow was upon his head, and his face was as it were the sun, and his feet as pillars of fire: And he had in his hand a little book open: and he set his right foot upon the sea, and his left foot on the earth.

– Revelation 10:1-2

Another mighty angel appears, who is standing on the sea and the earth. From the description, he comes from the throne of God. He is probably the angel of the Lord. An angel that comes with all the authority from God to bring the message and carry it out.

There are disagreements concerning Revelation 10 about the sea and earth or land, which we can settle here.

A sea is often not a good place, as God connects it with the wicked:

> *But the wicked are like the troubled sea, when it cannot rest, whose waters cast up mire and dirt.*
>
> **- Isaiah 57:20**

It was also a sign of foreign nations or Gentiles.

> *Therefore thus saith the Lord GOD; Behold, I am against thee, O Tyrus, and will cause many nations to come up against thee, as the sea causeth his waves to come up.*
>
> **- Ezekiel 26:3**

Patmos, which is in the Aegean Sea, is between modern-day Greece and Turkey. This sea is a part of the larger Mediterranean Sea. Was the angel standing on a literal sea and earth? No, he is standing on the symbolic Roman empire and Jerusalem.

The empire surrounded the whole of the Mediterranean Sea and known in Latin as *Mare Nostrum* ("Our Sea"); the Empire controlled the sea and also surrounded the earth of Jerusalem. Most Jews knew the empire as the sea and then makes sense when Jesus said:

> *Woe unto you, scribes and Pharisees, hypocrites! for ye compass sea and land to make one proselyte, and when he is made, ye make him twofold more the child of hell than yourselves.*
>
> **- Matthew 23:15**

This angel has authority over both the sea and land—symbolized by the right and left foot, and judgment will fall upon both, as increased destruction will fall upon the empire and Jerusalem.

John is holding a little book that will become Revelation. He hears of time no longer, or the OT temple age ending, but also the mystery of God revealed—the kingdom of God forever disclosed in Jewish and Gentile Spirit-baptized Christians.

> *And the angel which I saw stand upon the sea and upon the earth lifted up his hand to heaven, And sware by him that liveth for ever and ever, who created heaven, and the things that therein are, and the earth, and the things that therein are, and the sea, and the things which are therein, that there should be time no longer:*
>
> *But in the days of the voice of the seventh angel, when he shall begin to sound, the mystery of God should be finished, as he hath declared to his servants the prophets.*
>
> **– Revelation 10:5-7**

And the book of Ephesians confirms this mystery of God:

> *Having made known unto us the mystery of his will, according to his good pleasure which he hath purposed in himself: That in the dispensation of the fulness of times he might gather together in one all things in Christ, both which are in heaven, and which are on earth; even in him: I*
>
> *n whom also we have obtained an inheritance, being predestinated according to the purpose of him who worketh all things after the counsel of his own will: That we should be to the praise of his glory, who first trusted in Christ.*
>
> **– Ephesians 1:9-12**

And in Colossians…

> *To whom God would make known what is the riches of the glory of this mystery among the Gentiles; which is Christ in you, the hope of glory:*
>
> **– Colossians 1:27**

We now know this mystery is the Spirit of Christ, the hope of glory is within us.

In the beginning, Adam was supposed to eat of the Tree of Life, to receive the eternal Spirit of God. The serpent (Lucifer) deceived Eve into eating his fruit. When Adam saw Eve didn't die from touching or even eating of the fruit, it also deceived Adam to eat from the tree of knowledge of good and evil.

God maintained His Tree of Life mystery until Jesus made His kingdom's riches known to us through baptizing us in His Spirit.

John hears the voice from heaven again, who says to take and eat the little book. It is bittersweet. Bitter because the temple age is ending, but also sweet, since it reveals the mystery of God in those who trust Jesus.

And when he was demanded of the Pharisees, when the kingdom of God should come, he answered them and said, The kingdom of God cometh not with observation:
Neither shall they say, Lo here! or, lo there! for, behold, the kingdom of God is within you.

- Luke 17:20-21

Religious teachers today are making the same mistake the Jews did, thinking God was going to set up His kingdom *physically* on our earth. This was never the plan. After our baptism, we begin spiritually ruling in His kingdom, and will do so for eternity in the spirit realm.

The angel then tells John he will continue to prophesy to all the contents of this little book.

And he said unto me, Thou must prophesy again before many peoples, and nations, and tongues, and kings.

- Revelation 10:11

Revelation 11

And there was given me a reed like unto a rod: and the angel stood, saying, Rise, and measure the temple of God, and the altar, and them that worship therein.
But the court which is without the temple leave out, and measure it not; for it is given unto the Gentiles: and the holy city shall they tread under foot forty and two months.

– **Revelation 11:1-2**

Measuring the temple and altar is not to see how big they are (because it includes the worshipers), but John is measuring their value. They are corrupt beyond saving. The outer court will end up a spoil for the Gentiles.

In this rebuilt temple (the Babylonians destroyed the first one in 586 BC), it had sections for sacrifices and government, and a court divided out that the Gentiles used for their worship.

The temple had no value to God after the sacrifices offered became corrupt.

The time (v.2) verifies how long the first war on the holy city and the Jews occurred: forty-two months.

After the temple fell, the invaders stole the valuables from the desecrated temple and soon erected emblems to Titus, and worshiped him upon the eastern side of the court.

> *"And now the Romans, upon the flight of the seditious into the city, and upon the burning of the holy house itself, and of all the buildings round about it, brought their ensigns to the temple and set them over against its eastern gate; and there did they offer sacrifices to them, and there did they make Titus imperator with the greatest acclamations of joy."*
>
> (WOJ Book 6, Chapter 6.1)

Emperor Hadrian would later erect a statue of Jupiter in the court in approximately AD 133, which started the last Jewish revolt.

In AD 688, the Islamic religion built the Dome of the Rock upon the court, and this Gentile control still holds true today.

The next Revelation verses have caused much confusion in attempts to figure out what John meant concerning the two witnesses. It is fairly clear from reading different commentaries that no one knew for sure who the two witnesses are. This is because most scholars and others are trying to tie them to individuals, without understanding the scriptures from Zechariah and Paul's teaching in Romans chapter 11.

We need to remember again that John is in the spiritual realm, and now he sees these two olive trees recognizing them from OT history.

And I will give power unto my two witnesses, and they shall prophesy a thousand two hundred and threescore days, clothed in sackcloth.

These are the two olive trees, and the two candlesticks standing before the God of the earth.

– **Revelation 11:3-4**

Sackcloth represented a time of misery, and therefore the two witnesses found no pleasure in their prophecies.

God will give prophecy power to His two witnesses. This will allow them to prophecy for three and one-half years (1260 days).

But who are the two witnesses?

"These are the two olive trees, AND the two candlesticks standing before the God of the earth." This is an important clue.

It begins in the book from Zechariah.

And the angel that talked with me came again, and waked me, as a man that is wakened out of his sleep.

And said unto me, What seest thou? And I said, I have looked, and behold a candlestick all of gold, with a bowl upon the top of it, and his seven lamps thereon, and seven pipes to the seven lamps, which are upon the top thereof:

And two olive trees by it, one upon the right side of the bowl, and the other upon the left side thereof.

So I answered and spake to the angel that talked with me, saying, What are these, my lord?

Then the angel that talked with me answered and said unto me, Knowest thou not what these be? And I said, No, my lord.

Then he answered and spake unto me, saying, This is the word of the LORD *unto Zerubbabel, saying, Not by might, nor by power, but by my spirit, saith the* LORD *of hosts.*

- Zechariah 4:1-4

Any Jewish person who had entered the temple would have understood the candlestick to be the Menorah. Pure olive oil from the pipes lit the seven candles each day. This symbol represented certain things, such as the seven spirits of God, the seven days of creation, but particularly the light of the world as the word of God in the coming Messiah.

God would conquer evil not by might or power, but by His *Spirit*.

Then answered I, and said unto him, What are these two olive trees upon the right side of the candlestick and upon the left side thereof?
And I answered again, and said unto him, What be these two olive branches which through the two golden pipes empty the golden oil out of themselves?
And he answered me and said, Knowest thou not what these be? And I said, No, my lord. Then said he, These are the two anointed ones, that stand by the Lord of the whole earth.

- Zechariah 4:11-14

The olive trees are the same ones in Revelation. Zechariah saw two olive branches flowing into one candlestick. As we read in the beginning of Revelation, a candlestick represented a church. There was only one "church" (spirit of Mosaic Law) represented through the temple. But there is also the prophecy of the Holy Spirit ("but by my Spirit") feeding the candlestick and coming in the NT church, which will pass into the Gentiles.

We see in this chapter, there are two candlesticks represented as two olive trees. As the Zechariah chapter said, "these two are anointed, and stand by the Lord of the whole earth".

So, who are the two anointed ones? The two olive trees from two candlesticks are going to prophecy, and are the Jewish and the Gentile spirit baptized Christians! They are going to prophesy the destruction of unbelievers in the whole earth (Jerusalem and surrounding areas).

If we read Romans chapter 11, Paul gives an excellent teaching on the grafting in of the wild olive tree (Gentiles) into the original olive tree (representing the Jews). He shows the Jewish branches broken off, so that God could graft the Gentile branches in together.

Zechariah was seeing the prophecy, but he wasn't given the whole answer that we can now see—how the Jewish and Gentiles, or candlesticks, represented as olive trees, could feed the Holy Spirit golden oil word of God into one spirit baptized true church or become one candlestick.

If we can understand the spiritual aspect of this, we can understand:

And if any man will hurt them, fire proceedeth out of their mouth, and devoureth their enemies: and if any man will hurt them, he must in this manner be killed. (v 5)

The word "hurt" actually means: to do wrong or act wickedly towards (*Strong's* #91). When the true church (two witnesses comprising of Jews and Gentiles) testified of Jesus as the word of God (two-edged sword) it ticked off the unbelievers and they persecuted them. The other side of the sword brought judgment (fire) on the persecutors, causing their destruction.

These have power to shut heaven, that it rains not in the days of their prophecy: and have power over waters to turn them to blood, and to smite the earth with all plagues, as often as they will. (v 6)

Since the persecutors refused to listen, God shut off His Spirit to them (did not rain) and the waters (people) were slaughtered (to blood). The witness's testimony and prophecy brought the destruction through the plagues within the seven seals.

Next, we see the antichrist beast (most likely the Zealots) rise up to kill off the Jews and those who are prophesying the testimony of Jesus.

And when they shall have finished their testimony, the beast that ascendeth out of the bottomless pit shall make war against them, and shall overcome them, and kill them.
And their dead bodies shall lie in the street of the great city, which spiritually is called Sodom and Egypt, where also our Lord was crucified. And they of the people and kindreds and tongues and nations shall see their dead bodies three days and an half, and shall not suffer their dead bodies to be put in graves. (vv 7-10)

There are a few things we need to consider from these verses. We know the temple leaders hated those who converted into Christianity. The Romans (especially Caesar) hated them for not worshiping Rome or their idols. And, the Zealots hated them for not joining in the rebellion. Death came from everywhere.

"...Along all the roads also vast numbers of dead bodies lay in heaps, and even many of those that were so zealous in deserting at length chose rather to perish within the city; for the hopes of burial made death in their own city appear of the two less terrible to them. But these zealots came at last to that degree of barbarity, as not to bestow a burial either on those slain in the city, or on those that lay

along the roads; but as if they had made an agreement to cancel both the laws of their country and the laws of nature, and, at the same time that they defiled men with their wicked actions, they would pollute the Divinity itself also, they left the dead bodies to putrefy under the sun;...

Nay, the terror was so very great, that he who survived called them that were first dead happy, as being at rest already; as did those that were under torture in the prisons, declare, that, upon this comparison, those that lay unburied were the happiest.

These men, therefore, trampled upon all the laws of men, and laughed at the laws of God; and for the oracles of the prophets, they ridiculed them as the tricks of jugglers; yet did these prophets foretell many things concerning [the rewards of] virtue, and [punishments of] vice, which when these zealots violated, they occasioned the fulfilling of those very prophecies belonging to their own country; for there was a certain ancient oracle of those men, that the city should then be taken and the sanctuary burnt, by right of war, when a sedition should invade the Jews, and their own hand should pollute the temple of God. Now while these zealots did not [quite] disbelieve these predictions, they made themselves the instruments of their accomplishment.

WOJ Book 4, Chapter 6:3

We can imagine the joy the demons and Satan temporarily experienced, thinking they were defeating the word of God, the witnesses, and His spiritual plan for salvation.

And they that dwell upon the earth shall rejoice over them, and make merry, and shall send gifts one to another; because these two prophets tormented them that dwelt on the earth (v 10).

It is possible a grand slaughter took place during Passover. Along with the Feast of Bread convocation, there was also a spring festival called *Purim*. This came from the OT when the Jews

conquered their enemies who wanted to destroy them (Esther 9:21–22). During this celebration:
- They read from Esther in the OT.
- Gave money gifts to at least two poor people.
- Sent two kinds of food to at least one person.
- Celebrated with wine.

Jerusalem swelled with "people and kindred's, tongues and nations" to celebrate Purim and Feast of Bread. The demonic-infested Jews celebrated the witnesses' deaths during Purim.

> *And after three days and an half the spirit of life from God entered into them, and they stood upon their feet; and great fear fell upon them which saw them.*
>
> *And they heard a great voice from heaven saying unto them, Come up hither. And they ascended up to heaven in a cloud; and their enemies beheld them.*
>
> *And the same hour was there a great earthquake, and the tenth part of the city fell, and in the earthquake were slain of men seven thousand: and the remnant were affrighted, and gave glory to the God of heaven.*
>
> *– Revelation 11:13*

The devil's kingdom watched the witnesses get raptured or raised from the dead. All the Spirit baptized true church is raised to rule and reign with Jesus for eternity.

Believers are still the witnesses and take over on *our* earth. We are rulers and priests, ruling over the devil and demons, giving the testimony of Jesus—revealing the kingdom of God to all who will repent and receive Jesus and His Spirit baptism.

Revelation 12

As is perhaps obvious now, Revelation not only provides different perspectives of the judgment(s), but why they occurred. It also displays Babylonian Zodiac symbols used by the Romans contrasting with Biblical symbolism of the true church. It is now evident that there is no passage of time in the spirit realm—it is eternity.

Remember, John saw Jesus as the Lamb, Root of David, and the Lion of Judah. John is viewing what has already happened there, the cleansing of God's kingdom, and the earth (Jerusalem) will shortly experience the same outcome from these visions.

If we read Revelation knowing these are the spiritual events that took place beforehand, then we have a majestic view into the worst evil and deception imaginable, what God defeated for us in His kingdom.

Therefore, what we see in this chapter is a sweeping panoramic view from the beginning of the war in the spiritual realm when Lucifer tried to take over God's kingdom, to the kingdom restoration as a New Jerusalem through the true church.

For most of the male Jews, the symbolism and signs were nothing new. During their childhood, Jewish boys memorized at least the first five books (Torah) of our Bible, and would understand the symbolism. We can now see a unique vision, a powerful biblical symbolism in God's heaven or spiritual realm.

And there appeared a great wonder in heaven; a woman clothed with the sun, and the moon under her feet, and upon her head a crown of twelve stars,
And she being with child cried, travailing in birth, and pained to be delivered.

- **Revelation 12:1-2**

When we refer these verses to the beginnings of Genesis, this woman will give us a better understanding.

And I will put enmity between thee and the woman, and between thy seed and her seed; it shall bruise thy head, and thou shalt bruise his heel.

- **Genesis 3:15**

Lucifer-Satan will hate the woman. The woman will provide the seed to Jesus from the spiritual realm into the earth. Lucifer-Satan will try to kill or corrupt her seed. The moon represents Lucifer's seed, and the woman's seed by the crown of twelve stars.

The woman with the twelve stars symbolizes a birther, so to speak, with the twelve stars first symbolizing the birthing of the twelve spiritual patriarchs, then the stars as the twelve tribes of Israel, and then into the twelve disciples of the true church. Her feet always standing upon the pagan moon worship under her feet, and later contrasts with the red dragon in this chapter.

She is wrapped in the represented sun of righteousness.

But unto you that fear my name shall the Sun of righteousness arise with healing in his wings;

– Malachi 4:2

Then shall the righteous shine forth as the sun in the kingdom of their Father.

– Revelation 13:43

Righteousness has always separated evil from good. It always had the right to overcome evil committed by Lucifer-Satan.

The crown on her head symbolizes victory through the twelve stars, over the moon of religious pagan worship under her feet.

This vision of a woman with twelve stars caused many arguments, mainly from Babylonian or the Roman Catholic religion origins. Some teach it is Mary or the constellation Virgo or even the goddess Queen of Heaven.

Others claim the constellation Virgo was in place with the moon under her feet during the spiritual conception of Jesus.

What this chapter shows is how and why the seed of the true church came to our earth. We know God loved the Jewish people through OT covenants as His spiritual wife, whose lineage would bring Jesus into our world. Later, we will see the true church now as His bride, through the NT blood shed covenant with Jesus.

Beginning with Eve as the mother of all living, her seed, continuing with Seth as seed to Jesus, had *twelve* descendants or patriarchs (pre-flood as stars).

After the flood, the woman represents the *twelve* stars as the tribes of Israel, then delivering Jesus and the true church through *twelve* disciples.

The *red* dragon (Lucifer) caused the death of Abel. God told the serpent (red dragon) that from the seed of Eve would come his defeat (Genesis 3:15).

Abel, through faith, had provided a more excellent sacrifice to God (Hebrews 11:4). Cain did not—his came from the cursed ground without faith. Cain then killed Abel as a sacrifice to Lucifer because Lucifer thought God accepted Abel as the seed to Jesus.

A created being from God's creations caused the shedding of blood on the earth, and there was no equal covenant for this until the Lamb of God shed His blood on the earth to compensate for the evil.

Seeing that God would endlessly create a seed to Jesus, Lucifer determined to recruit as many followers as possible from his "seed" (fallen angels) and he deceived as many as possible away from God. He thought that if the seed of Eve would destroy him, he would have followers to corrupt the seed line (Genesis 6:1-5).

And there appeared another wonder in heaven; and behold a great red dragon, having seven heads and ten horns, and seven crowns upon his heads.

- Revelation 12:3

Before the flood, evil's direct descendants (ten horns, including Cain) were Enoch (not from Seth's line), Irad, Mehujael, Methushael, Lamech, Jabal, Jubal, Tubal-cain, and Naamah.

The twelve direct descendants as Patriarchs to Jesus (as stars, starting with Seth from Eve) were Enos, Cainan, Mahalaleel, Jared, Enoch, Methuselah, Lamech, Noah, Shem, Ham, and Japheth. They were all before the flood, with Noah, Shem, Ham, and Japheth, with their wives passing through into our world.

Lucifer's fallen angels and followers (a third of all beings) were also in the flood to our world. Lucifer tried to block the sacrifice from the Lamb of God, so God cast him to our earth as the fallen Satan.

And his tail drew the third part of the stars of heaven, and did cast them to the earth: and the dragon stood before the woman which was ready to be delivered, for to devour her child as soon as it was born.

– **Revelation 12:4**

The red dragon, now Satan in our world, had to start over with Nimrod, building seven cities/temples (heads) to spread Satan's deceptions from Babylon. These were Erech, Accad, and Calneh in Shinar, and through Asshur in Assyria, the cities of Nineveh, Rehoboth, Calah, and Resen. (Genesis 10:10–11)

The devil didn't know where or when the woman would deliver the child, so he flooded the earth with his pagan followers and then when she did, they could kill the child. Satan deceived Herod to kill the young Jewish boys after the birth of Jesus.

Then Herod, when he saw that he was mocked of the wise men, was exceeding wroth, and sent forth, and slew all the children that were in Bethlehem, and in all the coasts thereof, from two years old and under, according to the time which he had diligently inquired of the wise men.

– **Matthew 2:16**

The woman vision passes through the spirit realm into our world to birth the *twelve* tribes of Israel.

And God said unto him, I am God Almighty: be fruitful and multiply; a nation and a company of nations shall be of thee, and kings shall come out of thy loins;

- Genesis 35:11

Now the sons of Jacob were twelve:
The sons of Leah; Reuben, Jacob's firstborn, and Simeon, and Levi, and Judah, and Issachar, and Zebulun:
The sons of Rachel; Joseph, and Benjamin:
And the sons of Bilhah, Rachel's handmaid; Dan, and Naphtali:
And the sons of Zilpah, Leah's handmaid: Gad, and Asher: these are the sons of Jacob, which were born to him in Padanaram.

– Genesis 35:22-26

And [Joseph] dreamed yet another dream, and told it his brethren, and said, Behold, I have dreamed a dream more; and, behold, the sun and the moon and the eleven stars made obeisance to me.

– Genesis 37:9

For the Lord hath called thee as a woman forsaken and grieved in spirit, and a wife of youth, when thou wast refused, saith thy God.

– Isaiah 54:6

I have seen the travail, which God hath given to the sons of men to be exercised in it.

– Ecclesiastes 3:10

When the Spirit of God raises Jesus from the dead, He ascends to heaven, and His church disperses in the wilderness with only the Holy Spirit to feed and comfort her.

Seeing Jesus's resurrection to heaven, then later the two witnesses in mass ascend to heaven, Satan and his fallen angels attempt to follow. But Michael and his angels block them and cast them out *in* to the earth (vv. 7–9).

Therefore rejoice, ye heavens, and ye that dwell in them. Woe to the inhabiters of the earth and of the sea!
For the devil is come down unto you, having great wrath, because he knoweth that he hath but a short time.

— ***Revelation 12:12***

John sees another warning to the earth (Jerusalem) and the sea (Roman empire) that the devil will attack with great wrath for 1260 days (a short time).

John then sees Satan casting a flood out of his mouth (vv. 15–16). In the OT, a flood symbolizes Israel's enemies (Isaiah 59:19, Jeremiah 46:7).

The earth, and the Zealot people who started the war, took on the Romans. It is probably at this time or shortly before, the sealed of God (144,000) fled to the Pella wilderness, as some historians believe.

The earth (Jews battling Rome and others) could stand off their enemies for a while protecting the temple (v. 16).

The appointed place is Israel, or Jerusalem, where judgments for a time, times, and half a time occurred in AD 66, AD 70, and AD 132.

From the last verse (17), we know the dragon makes war (great tribulation) with the true church (rest of her offspring-bride) through today.

Don Nordstrom

Revelation 13

We already saw that a beast with seven heads, seven crowns, and ten horns was Lucifer in heaven and, now, Satan on earth.

> *And I stood upon the sand of the sea, and saw a beast rise up out of the sea, having seven heads and ten horns, and upon his horns ten crowns, and upon his heads the name of blasphemy.*
>
> *– Revelation 13:1*

John sees this Satanic beast rise out of the Roman Empire. There will soon be another beast rise from the earth (Jerusalem and temple). We next see the conquered Roman provinces:

> *And the beast which I saw was like unto a leopard, and his feet were as the feet of a bear, and his mouth as the mouth of a lion: and the dragon gave him his power, and his seat, and great authority.*
>
> *– Revelation 13:2*

This verse would have snapped the attention of hearers or readers back to the book of Daniel 7:3–10. This prophet experienced a similar vision of events during his time and in the future, the wars leading to the beast, Rome. Daniel then saw these wars with the conquerors.

The three creatures were in opposite order for Daniel looking forward, the kingdoms conquered in succession. He saw them as Babylon (lion), conquered by the Medo-Persians (bear), conquered by Greece (leopard), which the Roman Empire conquered.

His prophecy continued in more detail what would happen to the Jews and the temple from his time, leading to the temple destruction in AD 70.

Some scholars think Daniel is prophesying about our end time. There is a blank period in the Bible between Malachi and Matthew, and unless people study the history of the Jewish people during this time, they will not understand most of Daniel's prophecy was fulfilled during this period.

Now John is looking backward in history towards Daniel, seeing the conquered countries in reverse order. Again:

And the beast which I saw was like unto a leopard, and his feet were as the feet of a bear, and his mouth as the mouth of a lion: and the dragon gave him his power, and his seat, and great authority.

— ***Revelation 13:2***

Despite the world today, through false doctrines, looking for this supposed conquering antichrist beast in their lifetime, obviously this beast represented Rome (the empire).

John mentions *antichrist* four times in the NT, and each time, the antichrist already existed, there is more than one, it is a spirit, and many deceivers claiming Jesus Christ (the Messiah) had not come (1 John 2:18, 22; 4:3; and 2 John 1:7).

In the next verse from Revelation 13, John sees a "head" seem to suffer a deadly wound.

> *And I saw one of his heads as it were wounded to death; and his deadly wound was healed: and all the world wondered after the beast.*
>
> *- Revelation 13:3*

It would seem a deadly wound couldn't heal, but appears it did. Most Preterists, who believe Revelation concerns the judgment, also affirm this "head" is the Roman emperor Nero. The head concerns Nero, but not directly. There are two strong possibilities, which may combine to be one head.

Sometimes when we read a book we receive clues, but we need to read further to find out what the clues mean. This is true in Revelation, as the head here seems to define a Roman mountain but, later, also the mountains of Jerusalem.

> *And here is the mind which hath wisdom. The seven heads are seven mountains, on which the woman sitteth.*
>
> *- Revelation 17:9*

Rome is famous for having seven mountains or hills. If "seven heads" equals seven mountains, then one head equals one mountain or hill. In AD 64, most of Rome burned to the ground, including the Forum, where government activities took place. Many blamed Nero, and he blamed the Christians.

The fire destroyed at least one hill or mountain, Palatine. This is where the palace of Nero stood, along with senate homes and where the wealthy elite lived.

After the fire, it appeared to an outsider that Rome was dead, and the Roman government moved against Nero. However, the "wound" healed, thanks to Nero emptying the treasury to rebuild the city, Palatine, and his palace. After Nero rebuilt his palace, he placed his statue in the center of Rome.

Subsequently, Nero restored Rome to its former glory, and then he committed suicide (perhaps by a sword) in AD 68 to avoid execution by the government, thus ending the Julio-Claudian dynasty of Caesars (Revelation 13:4–10). Rome later came back with a vengeance under Vespasian and his son Titus.

Chaos and civil war broke out until Vespasian gained power. He was the beginning of the Flavian dynasty, who soon restored order healing the dynasty wound. Israel's destruction continued under Vespasian and Titus.

As we stated before, when Jesus was on our earth, He said little of Rome and its tyranny over the Jews. The temple leaders sent Jesus to His crucifixion, stating Caesar was their king.

But they cried out, Away with him, away with him, crucify him. Pilate saith unto them, Shall I crucify your King? The chief priests answered, We have no king but Caesar.

– John 19:15

The temple leaders forced their followers to worship the dragon-Satan, through Rome's gods and pagan images. The Jews witnessed the near end of Rome, but then saw it coming back to destroy them.

And they worshipped the dragon which gave power unto the beast: and they worshipped the beast, saying, Who is like unto the beast? Who is able to make war with him?

– Revelation 13:4

John just told us of the beast from the sea; now we will see the beast of the earth that rose up in the land of the Jews.

And I beheld another beast coming up out of the earth; and he had two horns like a lamb, and he spake as a dragon.

And he exerciseth all the power of the first beast before him, and causeth the earth and them which dwell therein to worship the first beast, whose deadly wound was healed. And he doeth great wonders, so that he taketh fire come down from heaven on the earth in the sight of men,

And deceiveth them that dwell on the earth by the means of those miracles which he had power to do in the sight of the beast; saying to them that dwell on the earth, that they should make an image to the beast, which had the wound by a sword, and did live.

And he had power to give life unto the image of the beast, that the image of the beast should both speak, and cause that as many as would not worship the image of the beast should be killed.

And he causeth all, both small and great, rich and poor, free and bond, to receive a mark in their right hand, or in their foreheads: And that no man might buy or sell, save he that had the mark, or the name of the beast, or the number of his name. Here is wisdom. Let him that hath understanding count the number of the beast: for it is the number of a man; and his number is Six hundred threescore and six.

– *Revelation 13:11–18*

The *666* number has captured the attention and imagination of many bestselling book writers. The world today assigns this number for political leaders, organizations, or religions. They claim this is the number of the future antichrist beast, all of which are from the false end-of-our-time doctrines.

However, John says this beast:
- comes up from the "earth", Jerusalem, the temple, or the surrounding area,
- has two horns like a lamb,
- speaks like a dragon (deceives),
- receives his power from Rome or Caesar (the first beast) and forces everyone to worship Caesar,
- brings fire (judgment) down from heaven,
- people cannot buy or sell without the beast's identity or image.

Many scholars of the Revelation judgment think the 666 number is Nero, but this man/beast is different. This beast came from the earth and (miraculously) caused the worship of Nero, Vespasian, or Rome, inclusive of the first beast.

There are a few possibilities for this earth beast, but we will nominate Herod Agrippa II. He was Jewish and at first appeared as a "lamb" or in favor of the Jews by beautifying Jerusalem and the temple, along with other towns. Nero gave him all power from Rome to rule over the temple and Jerusalem.

A horn symbolizes a king or ruler and since he was the second King Agrippa, he has two horns. Agrippa II was a puppet image of Nero, as king over Jerusalem.

Agrippa *spoke* and acted for Nero and as king over the Jews; he managed the temple activities, chose the high priest, and built or rebuilt parts of the city. He was in Nero's favor and caused the Jews to worship Rome's idols and Caesar.

In addition, he minted coins with his own face and Nero's face or image on it (came to life and image of the beast(s)). The Romans sometimes allowed the Jews to mint their own coins in their towns, but when travelers came to Jerusalem, they could only use the coins minted in Jerusalem. Money-changers in the temple exchanged foreign coins with the Jerusalem coins, with Agrippa's or Nero's image on them.

With Agrippa's as the only money in Jerusalem, no one could buy or sell without using one of his coins, which the images on them represented the beasts.

Part of the temple acted as a government center, where the scribes documented transactions (most were debts) for the Jews and for Rome. The scribes then rolled these official documents up like a scroll, sealed them with wax, and then imprinted them with a signet ring from the king, now Agrippa II.

> *Write ye also for the Jews, as it liketh you, in the king's name, and seal it with the king's ring: for the writing which is written in the king's name, and sealed with the king's ring, may no man reverse.*
>
> *– Esther 8:8*

The Jews could not do official business without the seal from Agrippa's signet ring. Whatever the case, the Jews knew that by obeying and using the coins of Agrippa/Nero, or worshiping the temple idol religion run by Agrippa, they were in effect acknowledging the beast(s) as a king or a god.

In order to function with peace and security in the Roman Empire, people had to have the right mindset. Agrippa was the appointed king over the Jews, and made sure they knew who their god(s) were, and worshiped only them. (Forehead or mind marked with idol knowledge and hand marked with action of worship).

But many Christians refused to honor Agrippa, Rome, Nero, or any of their idols as kings or gods. Nero would then send them into his circus and tortured them to their deaths.

In AD 64, Nero had appointed Gessius Florus procurator of Judea. Later, Florus with Roman troops stormed into Jerusalem, robbing the temple treasury for supposed Roman taxes. Agrippa tried to appease the Jews but caused literal "fire" down upon the high priest, King Agrippa, and his sister Bernice, when the Jews rioted. The Zealot group, Sicarii, encouraged the rioting when they overpowered King Agrippa's soldiers, and freed the Jews of their debts, starting the uprising towards the first revolt.

> "And when they had joined to themselves many of the Sicarii, who crowded in among the weaker people, [that was the name for such robbers as had under their bosoms swords called Sicae,] they grew bolder, and carried their undertaking further; insomuch that the king's soldiers were overpowered by their multitude and boldness; and so they gave way, and were driven out of the upper city by force.
>
> The others then set fire to the house of Ananias the high priest, and to the palaces of Agrippa and Bernice; after which they carried the fire to the place where the archives were reposited, and made haste to burn the contracts belonging to their creditors, and thereby to dissolve their obligations for paying their debts;
>
> and this was done in order to gain the multitude of those who had been debtors, and that they might persuade the poorer sort to join in their insurrection with safety against the more wealthy; so the keepers of the records fled away, and the rest set fire to them."
>
> (WOJ Book 2, Chapter 17.6)

After the Sicarii destroyed the documents with all the debt obligations, this, in turn, encouraged the Jewish revolt with their enemies.

The Jews were at first successful at driving the elite (kings) and Romans out of Jerusalem. Agrippa II fled Jerusalem and later joined the Roman general Titus's army, attacking the towns and villages in Judea and his own people.

Whether the 666 number calculates as Agrippa II or to Nero is not important to us, but would have been to hearers of Revelation in John's time.

Revelation 14

The first five verses bring out the 144,000 again from Revelation, chapter 7. They were the first (fruits) to receive the seal of the Holy Spirit from God, and then the gentiles. They sing the new song of the gospel of Christ in the kingdom of God.

> *In whom ye also trusted, after that ye heard the word of truth, the gospel of your salvation: in whom also after that ye believed, ye were sealed with that holy Spirit of promise.*
>
> *– Ephesians 1:1*

In addition, the first seven verses of Revelation 14 relate to Acts 2, when many nations heard the apostles teach, and the gospel of Jesus daily converted thousands of listeners.

There was a new belief system in town—one that did not require pagan or temple worship (sometimes with the pagan (Jezebel) prostitutes). This new belief would reveal the Holy Spirit into their lives as virgin Christians. Verses 6 and 8 contrast two angel messages.

The angel in verse 6:

> *And I saw another angel fly in the midst of heaven, having the everlasting gospel to preach unto them that dwell on the earth, and to every nation, and kindred, and tongue, and people.*
>
> *– Revelation 14:6*

And the angel in verse 8:

> *And there followed another angel, saying, Babylon is fallen, is fallen, that great city, because she made all nations drink of the wine of the wrath of her fornication.*
>
> *– Revelation 14:8*

The gods, goddesses, idols, and rituals, which started from Babylon, held the nations in the "wrath of her fornication". The Jewish temple leaders brought in this symbolism (Mystery Babylon) and allowed worship or sacrifices to the idols or emperors of Rome.

Despite the work of the apostles and warnings from prophets throughout the OT, the Jewish people still did not believe God would destroy them for their idol worship.

By following the Roman system of worship inspired from Babylon, there was relative peace, prosperity, and security. However, without the Holy Spirit, judgment from the judge in heaven condemned them.

> *And the third angel followed them, saying with a loud voice, If any man worship the beast and his image, and receive his mark in his forehead, or in his hand, The same shall drink of the wine of the wrath of God,*

which is poured out without mixture into the cup of his indignation; and he shall be tormented with fire and brimstone in the presence of the holy angels, and in the presence of the Lamb: And the smoke of their torment ascendeth up for ever and ever: and they have no rest day nor night, who worship the beast and his image, and whosoever receiveth the mark of his name.

- Revelation 14:9-11

Those who were willful and purposely worshiped the kings or emperors with their idols suffered endless fire (judgment) and brimstone (torment).

And I heard a voice from heaven saying unto me, Write, Blessed are the dead which die in the Lord from henceforth: Yea, saith the Spirit, that they may rest from their labours; and their works do follow them.

- Revelation 14:13

As we will show later, when we receive the Holy Spirit, we (our spirit) are at once resting with God. Those who died before the NT Spirit-baptism stayed in the grave (hell–their spirits either with or without protection from Abraham) until Jesus came and resurrected them (Luke 16:24, Matthew 27:52–53). But when we are spirit-baptized now, we receive the kingdom of God, and through our spiritual gifts, we obtain rewards for our service through the gift (Matthew 25:15-29).

And I looked, and behold a white cloud, and upon the cloud one sat like unto the Son of man, having on his head a golden crown, and in his hand a sharp sickle.
And another angel came out of the temple, crying with a loud voice to him that sat on the cloud, Thrust in thy sickle, and reap: for

the time is come for thee to reap; for the harvest of the earth is ripe. And he that sat on the cloud thrust in his sickle on the earth; and the earth was reaped.

And another angel came out of the temple which is in heaven, he also having a sharp sickle.

And another angel came out from the altar, which had power over fire; and cried with a loud cry to him that had the sharp sickle, saying, Thrust in thy sharp sickle, and gather the clusters of the vine of the earth; for her grapes are fully ripe.

And the angel thrust in his sickle into the earth, and gathered the vine of the earth, and cast it into the great winepress of the wrath of God.

And the winepress was trodden without the city, and blood came out of the winepress, even unto the horse bridles, by the space of a thousand and six hundred furlongs.

– **Revelation 14:13-20**

It is apparent in this and the next chapter, Jesus first cleansed the spiritual realm and temple in Jerusalem. The angels come out of the temple and altar in heaven, one to destroy the spiritual earth, and the other to destroy the idol worshiping beings.

This is another perspective of Jerusalem's destruction. Jesus had left on a cloud after His resurrection, and now returns on a cloud of judgment and wrath. God symbolized Israel as His vineyard and field, and there is a temple wall decorated with grapes.

For the vineyard of the Lord of hosts is the house of Israel, and the men of Judah his pleasant plant: and he looked for judgment, but behold oppression; for righteousness, but behold a cry.

– **Isaiah 5:7**

"But that gate which was at this end of the first part of the house was, as we have already observed, all over covered with gold, as was its whole
wall about it; it had also golden vines above it, from which clusters of grapes hung as tall as a man's height."
(WOJ Book 5, Chapter 5.4)

Sixteen hundred furlongs are equal to about 200 miles or 50 square miles (space), which was about the area of Jerusalem. The total bloodshed from the infighting and from the Roman military spattered as high as the conquering horse's bridles.

Don Nordstrom

Revelation 15

Revelation 15 begins with showing seven angels with seven plagues, which are the fullness of His wrath (v. 1). It then shows the first redeemed who sang the song of Moses (OT) and now the song of the Lamb (NT) (vv. 2–4).

These are the Spirit-baptized Jews who listened to the apostles and others. They had the peace of God (sea of glass) while they went through the tribulation judgment (mingled with fire). This chapter contrasts with the next chapter.

The wrath of God first cleanses the spiritual realm (smoke from the glory of God) and then in the next chapter the fulfillment of His wrath spills out onto the defiant Jews who refused to repent.

Don Nordstrom

Revelation 16

We again witness the false Jews' destruction as vials of wrath pour out onto Jerusalem, the temple, and throughout the sea. This is another perspective from what we saw before, but this is the completion of the (seven vials) total wrath.

The Jews became angry at their "sore" treatment, after worshiping the beast of Rome and allowing Babylonian rituals in their temple. Those involved in the war in both the earth and the sea either suffered their destruction by the rebels or slaughtered in the empire by the Roman armies (vv. 1–3).

> *"It had been proper indeed for us to have conjectured at the purpose of God much sooner, and at the very first, when we were so desirous of defending our liberty, and when we received such sore treatment from one another, and worse treatment from our enemies, and to have been sensible that the same God, who had of old taken the Jewish nation into his favor, had now condemned them to destruction;*

for had he either continued favorable, or been but in a lesser degree displeased with us, he had not overlooked the destruction of so many men, or delivered his most holy city to be burnt and demolished by our enemies."

(WOJ Book 7, Chapter 8.6)

The empire, rivers, and fountains filled with dead bodies (vv. 4–7).

"Now this destruction that fell upon the Jews, as it was not inferior to any of the rest in itself, so did it still appear greater than it really was; and this, because not only the whole country through which they fled was filled with slaughter, and Jordan could not be passed over, by reason of the dead bodies that were in it, but because the lake Asphaltites [Dead Sea] was also full of dead bodies, that were carried down into it by the river."

(WOJ Book 4, Chapter 7.6)

Within the burning villages and Jerusalem, the dead bodies were piling up from the catapults, hurling fiery stones and of those whom the rebels or kings slaughtered or starved by destroying their stores of food.

Despite all the "sores of plagues" of destruction throughout the empire, and Jerusalem on fire, the Jews refused to repent and tried to escape throughout the empire to their demise (vv. 8–11).

Through the rest of Revelation 16, previously in history, the Persian King, Cyrus, had diverted the Euphrates River to "dry it up" so his armies could march into and conquer Babylon. When Cyrus allowed the Jews to return to Jerusalem, the "kings" of Jerusalem later brought back their Babylonian worship into the rebuilt temple.

However, many Jews with their kings stayed behind in Babylon and flourished.

It is probable these eastern Jewish kings (kings of the east–v. 12), among others, were deceived (vv. 13-16) and traveled across the Euphrates, joined with the Zealots, to battle their enemies at the valley of Armageddon.

Frogs were detestable, unclean, such as the plague sent to Pharaoh in the OT, and represent much of the false prophecy coming from the mouths of the dragon, the rebels, and the Zealot John. God gives us a marvelous view, whereas we might physically see the false prophets, but behind them are spirits of the beast (antichrist) and the dragon, the devil.

Jerusalem divided into thirds (v. 19) with the armies of Galileans, Idumeans, and Zealots. They would later somewhat unite against the onslaught of the Romans, but were too late.

Armageddon is where the Israelites fought many battles with their enemies. Some religions teach Armageddon is an event in the future, but throughout OT history, innumerable Jews and their enemies died there.

Many countries came together to kill off the escaping Jews, and the Jews from the east (Babylon) at Armageddon, and it represents the battles with the land and sea.

Again, we see the hail of fiery stones from the catapults, and every village (island) and their temples or synagogues (mountains) destroyed in Israel.

Restored (Mystery) Babylon (Jerusalem) happened because the gold cup of her religions and ritualistic worship dominated the temple and Jerusalem. As we learned, these mystic beliefs have invaded our world and are still alive and well—deceiving the world today.

Don Nordstrom

Revelation 17

Israel and the Jews had so much promise. God promised them a prosperous life of peace and abundance, yet they worshiped idols and graven images, which only brought perdition (destruction) upon them and their temple.

The woman, "the great whore", in this chapter is the Mystery Babylon in the temple, Jerusalem, and kings of the earth now arrayed in the worship of Babylon. These rulers had a hand in the brutal murder of the witnesses (martyrs) for Jesus.

And the woman was arrayed in purple and scarlet colour, and decked with gold and precious stones and pearls,
having a golden cup in her hand full of abominations and filthiness of her fornication:

Revelation 17:4

Within the temple, there was a veil or curtain, and instead of the temple symbols for God and His kingdom, the leaders filled it with Babylonian symbols of idols—as Josephus points out the mystic meanings of these symbols:

> *It was a Babylonian curtain, embroidered with blue, and fine linen, and scarlet, and purple, and of a contexture that was truly wonderful.*
>
> Nor was this mixture of colors without its **mystical** interpretation, but was a kind of image of the universe; for by the scarlet there seemed to be enigmatically signified fire, by the fine flax the earth, by the blue the air, and by the purple the sea; two of them having their colors the foundation of this resemblance; but the fine flax and the purple have their own origin for that foundation, the earth producing the one, and the sea the other.
>
> This curtain had also embroidered upon it all that was **mystical** in the heavens, excepting that of the [twelve] signs, representing living creatures...
>
> Now the seven lamps signified the seven planets; for so many there were springing out of the candlestick. Now the twelve loaves that were upon the table signified the circle of the zodiac and the year; but the altar of incense, by its thirteen kinds of sweet-smelling spices with which the sea replenished it, signified that God is the possessor of all things that are both in the uninhabitable and habitable parts of the earth, and that they are all to be dedicated to his use."
>
> (emphasis added)
> (WOJ Book 5, Chapter 5.5)

These colors of the Mystery Babylonian belief system would enter the revived Roman empire, or Roman Catholic Church, and many symbols passed down and blended into organized religions today.

In the wisdom of God, the temple and city became Babylon, and the kings supported Babylon, including Rome, who brought their worship into the temple.

Many interpret the next verse as Rome or the Catholic Church on the seven mountains.

> *And here is the mind which hath wisdom. The seven heads are seven mountains, on which the woman sitteth.*
>
> *– Revelation 17:9*

However, Jerusalem has seven mountains or hills also, as Jerusalem itself sits on one of them. These are Mount Scopus, Olivet, Mount of Corruption, Ophel, the original Mount Zion, the New Mount Zion, and the Antonia Fortress Hill. This woman acts as the false worship, the "whore of Mystery Babylon".

The next verses remind us of the Herodian "kings".

> *And there are seven kings: five are fallen, and one is, and the other is not yet come; and when he cometh, he must continue a short space.*
> *And the beast that was, and is not, even he is the eighth, and is of the seven, and goeth into perdition.*
>
> *– Revelation 17:10-11*

This beast is again, King Agrippa II. The first king from the Herodian dynasty was Herod the Great, followed by Antipas, Philip I, Philip II, Agrippa I, and Agrippa II. The verse says there are seven kings, yet we only see six. However, five have fallen, and this would be Herod the Great through Agrippa I.

The one not yet come would be Gessius Florus, whom Nero appointed "king of Judea". Florus did not last long (a short space) as the procurator and, therefore, is the seventh.

The Zealots forced Agrippa II (one is and who was) with his sister out of Jerusalem. He then became a leader or king (the eighth) in Rome's army to destroy (perdition) the Jews. Therefore, King Agrippa II is "the beast that was, and is not, even he is the eighth, and is of the seven, and goeth into perdition".

And the ten horns which thou sawest are ten kings, which have received no kingdom as yet; but receive power as kings one hour with the beast.

- Revelation 17:12

The ten horns are most likely ten military legions or generals of Rome who the beast, Agrippa with Titus, joined together because: These have one mind, and shall give their power and strength unto the beast.

These shall make war with the Lamb, and the Lamb shall overcome them: for he is Lord of lords, and King of kings: and they that are with him are called, and chosen, and faithful.

And he saith unto me, The waters which thou sawest, where the whore sitteth, are peoples, and multitudes, and nations, and tongues.

And the ten horns which thou sawest upon the beast, these shall hate the whore, and shall make her desolate and naked, and shall eat her flesh, and burn her with fire.

For God hath put in their hearts to fulfil his will, and to agree, and give their kingdom unto the beast, until the words of God shall be fulfilled.

And the woman which thou sawest is that great city, which reigneth over the kings of the earth.

- Revelation 17:13-18

The Roman military, and others, hated the Jews in Jerusalem (the woman-whore), for example, from what the rebels were doing to the city. Jerusalem was a beautiful city before the revolt, with white marble walls, and the temple was huge with doors layered in gold and would have been spectacular to gaze upon even today.

Although it may appear the Lamb did not overcome the beast, He had in the spiritual realm, (but by my Spirit) and conquered Lucifer in heaven because now He is King of Kings and Lord of Lords. Satan cannot conquer the kingdom of God in our lives.

We need to realize His eternal kingdom is within Spirit-baptized believers, who are now the faithful rulers and priests.

The whore (Jerusalem), "that great city", sat within (or upon) the beast of the empire (until its destruction) and the Jewish kings had reined in its "earth".

How doth the city sit solitary, that was full of people! how is she become as a widow! she that was great among the nations, and princess among the provinces, how is she become tributary!

– **Lamentations 1:1**

Don Nordstrom

Revelation 18

This chapter continues with a great lament of the destruction of Jerusalem, the whore of Babylon. People would come from all nations to Jerusalem for the festivals and sacrifices.

At one time, Jerusalem was a storehouse of riches, and merchants came to trade in her wares. The kings and rulers became rich yet served her strange gods, while the Jewish citizens lived in poverty.

However, now she is desolate. She has gone up in flames and smoke, which was visible around the empire, and darkened the sun, moon, and stars. The remnant armies stole the valuables from the temple and city. The bride (true church) and groom (Jesus) were no longer there.

As with the seven churches at the start of Revelation, we need to discover how the wares of Mystery Babylon have enriched us with her deceptions. Her false religious beliefs, rules, and doctrines have crept into the religions and societies of the world. We have to eliminate (come out of) every belief that conflicts with the Word and kingdom of God.

We then see the main reason Jerusalem-Babylon met her downfall.

> *And in her was found the blood of prophets, and of saints, and of all that were slain upon the earth.*
>
> – ***Revelation 18:24***

Revelation 19

In this chapter, we see John contrast "the great whore" . . .

> *For true and righteous are his judgments: for he hath judged the great whore, which did corrupt the earth with her fornication, and hath avenged the blood of his servants at her hand.*
>
> – **Revelation 19:2**

. . .with the NT true church (bride, or wife).

> *Let us be glad and rejoice, and give honour to him: for the marriage of the Lamb is come, and his wife hath made herself ready. And to her was granted that she should be arrayed in fine linen, clean and white: for the fine linen is the righteousness of saints.*
>
> *And he saith unto me, Write, Blessed are they which are called unto the marriage supper of the Lamb. And he saith unto me, These are the true sayings of God.*
>
> – **Revelation 19:7-9**

God has judged and divorced the great whore. Now He presents His new bride, clothed in righteousness, making herself ready by the washing of her sins and with the baptism of His Spirit.

His Word of God (vs 13) goes throughout the world, dividing and conquering the deceiving Mystery Babylon with the true Word of God. All the spirits of the true church reign in heaven and are now ruling with God.

Before Jesus came and rose from the dead, the only people who knew about the uncreated God were the Jews (some Gentiles converted to Judaism). The Gentiles only knew about the Babylonian–inspired gods and goddesses, whom Satan spread their knowledge within his temples throughout the kingdoms as adopted gods and they received new names of worship.

However, the Jewish temple leaders were not faithful to their true God, as they called Caesar their king and continued worshiping the Babylonian idols. When the apostles tried to teach them the promised Savior from the OT was Jesus, they suffered tortures and death.

The Romans rarely buried their dead. The warring countries left thousands upon thousands (some say millions) of their warriors and dead Jews within Jerusalem, and around the Armageddon countryside for the fowl to consume flesh from the bones (vv 17,18).

At the end of the revolt, the false prophets in Jerusalem went to their eternal demise in Rome.

We need to remember the Word of God is a two-edged sword. It brings us to the knowledge and acceptance of His plan of salvation or to eternal judgment (fire) and the tormenting brimstone (lake of fire) without God.

Revelation 20

Revelation 20 introduces us to "a thousand years". Despite Revelation being full of symbolism, this term has confused the religionists to no end. Most have ignored these thousand years as symbolism and coined the term *millennium* to describe an actual one thousand years. The claim is Jesus will rule on our earth for a thousand years. This is not the case.

We will see once again; it is symbolism and generally means an *indefinite period or amount of totality*. It is the true church or "times of the Gentiles" age currently ruling on earth and not deceived by Mystery Babylon. Some examples where God used "a thousand(s)" symbolism from the OT:

And Moses chose able men out of all Israel, and made them heads over the people, rulers of thousands, rulers of hundreds, rulers of fifties, and rulers of tens.

– Exodus 18:25

And shewing mercy unto thousands of them that love me, and keep my commandments.

— **Exodus 20:6**

For every beast of the forest is mine, and the cattle upon a thousand hills.

— **Psalm 50:10**

He hath remembered his covenant for ever, the word which he commanded to a thousand generations.

— **Psalm 105:8**

Let's see what it means in Revelation.

And I saw an angel come down from heaven, having the key of the bottomless pit and a great chain in his hand.
And he laid hold on the dragon, that old serpent, which is the Devil, and Satan, and bound him a thousand years,
And cast him into the bottomless pit, and shut him up, and set a seal upon him, that he should deceive the nations no more, till the thousand years should be fulfilled: and after that he must be loosed a little season.
And I saw thrones, and they sat upon them, and judgment was given unto them: and I saw the souls of them that were beheaded for the witness of Jesus, and for the word of God, and which had not worshipped the beast, neither his image, neither had received his mark upon their foreheads, or in their hands; and they lived and reigned with Christ a thousand years.
But the rest of the dead lived not again until the thousand years were finished. This is the first resurrection.

> *Blessed and holy is he that hath part in the first resurrection: on such the second death hath no power, but they shall be priests of God and of Christ, and shall reign with him a thousand years.*
>
> **- Revelation 20:1-6**

This thousand-year age has gone on since the apostle Paul started converting Gentiles into the kingdom of God.

What we also need to remember from Revelation and the NT is once we get the baptism of His Holy Spirit, we are now true priests, our spirits judging and ruling with Jesus in His kingdom for eternity (the first resurrection).

> *Even when we were dead in sins, hath quickened us together with Christ, (by grace ye are saved;) And hath raised us up together, and made us sit together in heavenly places in Christ Jesus: That in the ages to come he might shew the exceeding riches of his grace in his kindness toward us through Christ Jesus.*
>
> **- Ephesians 2:5-7**

When Spirit-baptized people die, they immediately go into His spiritual kingdom because their names are in His Book of Life.

> *We are confident, I say, and willing rather to be absent from the body, and to be present with the Lord.*
>
> **- 2 Corinthians 5:8**

Those who die without the Spirit of God indwelling in them, will remain dead until the end, when Jesus raises them from their graves for their judgment of eternal life with God, or not.

Armageddon is where thousands upon thousands of Jews and soldiers died in battle and their bones were not buried, and then recall the Jews regaining Israel in 1948. Ezekiel 37 prophesied these events.

The dragon is loosed for a season, surrounding Israel again with hostile countries. There is growing antisemitism (hatred of Jews) more each day. He will deceive these nations to attack the Jews in Israel once again. This time however, God will save all those who call upon His name, and then the final judgment.

There is only one thing Jesus is waiting for, and that is our prayers to move God to bring His final judgment upon Mystery Babylon. Our great tribulation will continue until we do.

Revelation 21-22

The final two chapters describe the restored kingdom of God, filled with the new Jerusalem or spirit baptized true church. We will exist forever with God in the spiritual realm (New Heaven) on His restored or New Earth.

Most religions teach Jesus will literally reign *physically* on our earth for a thousand years, and this chapter shows this is not the case. God destroys our universe and earth along, with the wicked people left here. The saved will live in God's restored new heaven and new earth.

It is noted in the first verse that there is no more sea, which there was at one time in His kingdom. These were the fallen angels and spirits that warred against God in His original heaven and earth. They are cast out and have their eternal home in the now sea of the lake of fire (judgment).

There are several verses that describe the end of our universe which Bible teachers ignore.

But the heavens and the earth, which are now, by the same word are kept in store, reserved unto fire against the day of judgment and perdition of ungodly men.

- 2 Peter 3:7

But the day of the Lord will come as a thief in the night; in the which the heavens shall pass away with a great noise, and the elements shall melt with fervent heat, the earth also and the works that are therein shall be burned up.

- 2 Peter 3:10

Heaven and earth shall pass away, but my words shall not pass away.

- Matthew 24:35

John sees the new heaven and new earth, which are in God's world, or His heaven/universe. We will spend eternity restoring His world (v. 5), which Lucifer tried to destroy in darkness (v. 8). The new church now is like the New Jerusalem, as His bride.

The shape of the restored throne room is a huge cube, 1,500 miles long, 1,500 miles wide, and 1,500 miles high. There is a wall with many precious stones, and is about 216 feet with twelve gates, representing the twelve tribes of Israel, and in the foundation are the names of the twelve apostles.

We are the temple as the New Jerusalem, and there is no longer any night there. The darkness and destruction of Lucifer are gone. On God's restored earth, there are restored nations, and the kings of the nations bring glory to God.

Eternal life and healing flows forever from the throne of God, and the true church will reign forever.

Once again, the angel tells John the things shown to him are coming shortly and quickly.

> *And he said unto me, These sayings are faithful and true: and the Lord God of the holy prophets sent his angel to shew unto his servants the things which must shortly be done.*
>
> *Behold, I come quickly: blessed is he that keepeth the sayings of the prophecy of this book.*

– Revelation 22:6-7

There is no doubt the book of Revelation was for the seven churches identified in this book. It was a warning not to accept the Satan inspired Babylonian blend of worship. It is the promise of a restored heaven and earth from Genesis.

These seven churches would soon witness what happened to Jerusalem and the temple for acting as a whore and harlot towards God.

We now know of the deceptions from Mystery Babylon and need to bring this warning to all in our world today, because hostile nations are surrounding Israel again. There will be no warning this time of the final judgment.

Don Nordstrom

So Now What?

Thousands of organized religions have brought Roman-inspired festivals and Babylonian rituals into their churches and into our families. It is from these inspired Roman beliefs that the true church suffered tortures and death throughout the "thousand years" church age, because they refused to worship false doctrines from man and idols in religions.

We can come together and bring these things to the attention of our churches. We know the Holy Spirit individually guides the baptized true church into all truth, and we do not intend to tell people what to do. However, we can bring others into the conversation this book presents, starting with teaching about the risen Jesus and receiving His Holy Spirit.

In addition, we can quit lying to our children about the Tooth Fairy, the Easter Bunny, Santa Claus, and dinosaurs roaming our earth millions of years ago. Instead, we can teach there is a real kingdom here and now, with a real King, and our children are true princes and princesses, learning how to become priests and rulers with God. Perhaps then, when they become teenagers, they will quit rebelling against their lying parents and trust that they are learning the truth.

We can also point out how Babylonian inspired religious temples, emblems, icons, idols, carvings, and the like surround all of us to lead us away from our true–uncreated God.

It was the same for the Jews in the Roman Empire, as the Romans surrounded them with their Babylonian inspired idols and temples, which led many away from their true God.

When we discover how the world exists in almost total deception, it will seem like we are a drop in the ocean or a mustard seed attempting to grow in the desert. But we can overcome, as Jesus instructed us to do.

Once again, the world is deceived into Mystery Babylon. Satan inspired hostile enemies surround Israel, and it is just a short time before they act, bringing God's final judgment. We need to move now to warn as many as possible and bring them into the kingdom of God today.

Too many people are waiting to see a false prophet, antichrist, and seven-year agreement arise with Israel. These same people are eating, drinking, and making merry, and thinking after they see these things, they will perhaps get right with Jesus during His thousand-year reign on earth. We now know these are all false doctrines from Mystery Babylon to lead people to their destruction.

May the Holy Spirit inspire and reveal the truth to all who read this book.

Acknowledgments

Book Editing Associates: Floyd Largent
Liz Smith of InkSmithEditing.com

(This book is a revision from the original work these editors performed. They are not responsible for any errors in this revised book).

The author is retired but continues his 40-year research into history, especially Jewish history concerning the Bible. If there are questions or comments concerning this book, he is available by email at:

TheDesertPG@protonmail.com

If you enjoyed this book, please tell others and an online review would be *greatly* appreciated. Thank you for reading:
THE REVELATION HAPPENED.

1 Charles Darwin, letter (1882) to William Ogle, in Francis Darwin (ed.), *Life and Letters of Charles Darwin* (London: John Murray, 1887), 3:252.

2 Marco Polo, *The Travels of Marco Polo* (New York: Signet Classics, 1961), 158–159.

3 www.gutenberg.org